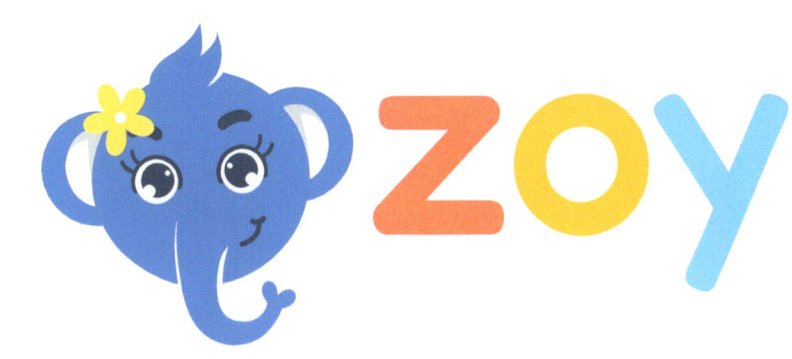

Social-Emotional Learning Kids Enjoy

Copyright © 2023 by Zoy LLC

All rights reserved. No parts of this book may be reproduced, stored in a retrieval system, or transmitted in any form or by any means, without prior written permission of the publisher, except in the case of brief quotations embedded in critical articles or reviews.

Every effort has been made in the preparation of this book to ensure the accuracy of the information presented. However, the information contained in this book is sold without warranty, either express or implied. Neither Zoy LLC nor its dealers and distributors will be held liable for any damages caused or alleged to have been caused directly or indirectly by this book.

Books published by Zoy LLC are available at special discounts for bulk purchases in the United States by corporations, institutions, and other organizations. For more information, please reach out to our Customer Service via email at hi@meetzoy.com.

First published: December 2023

Published by Zoy LLC
1050 Kettner Blvd, Suite B #1019
San Diego, CA, 92101
USA
www.meetzoy.com

Paperback ISBN: 978-1-962542-99-9
Ebook ISBN: 978-1-963310-00-9

Library of Congress Control Number: 2023923327

# Zoy's Joyful Jump

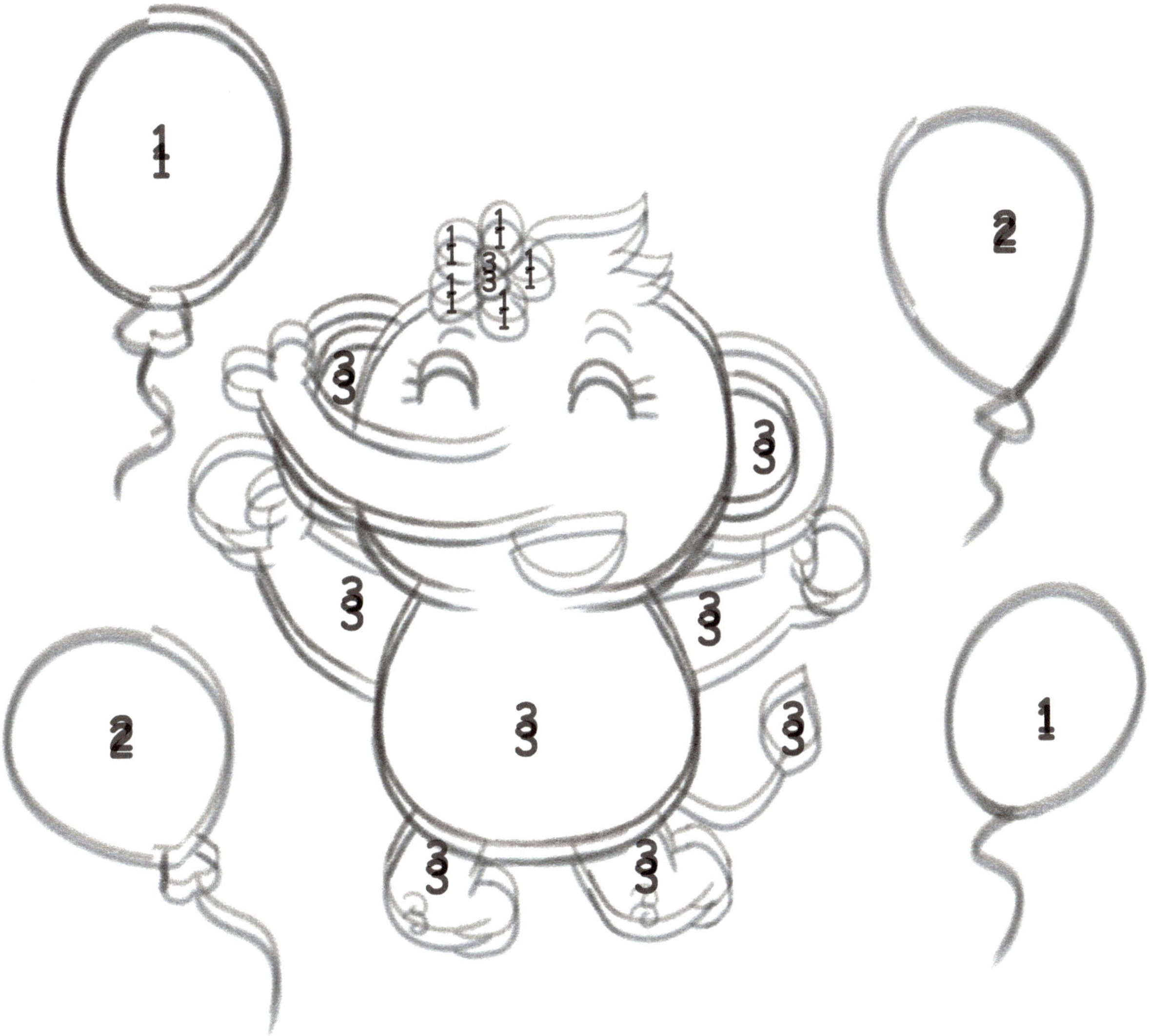

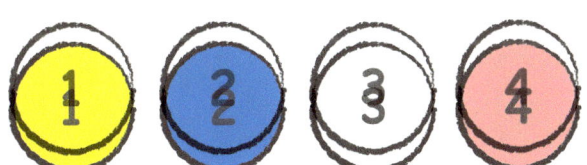

# Zoy's Sorrowful Sit

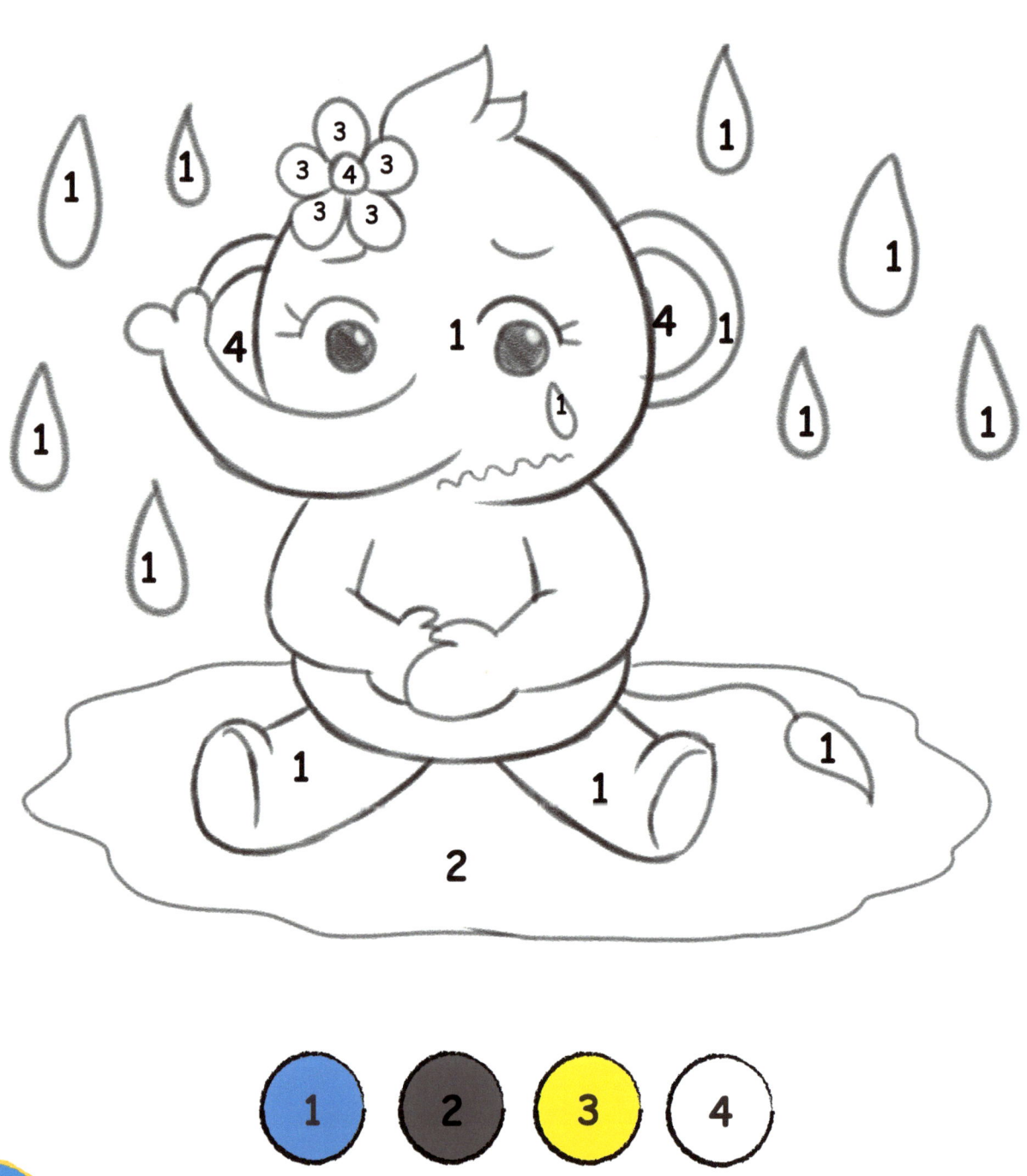

# Zoy's Energetic Excitement

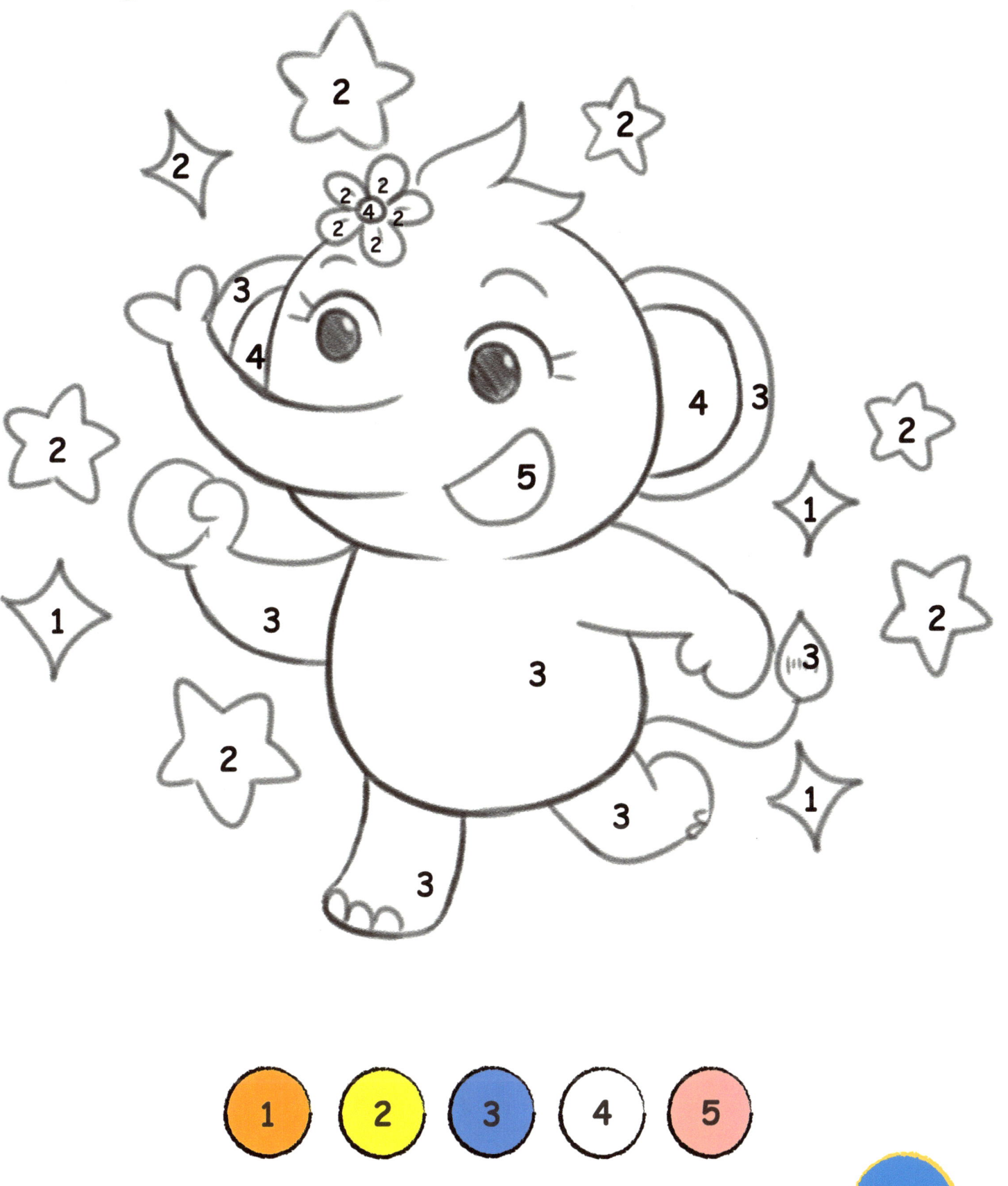

# Zoy's Calming Cloud

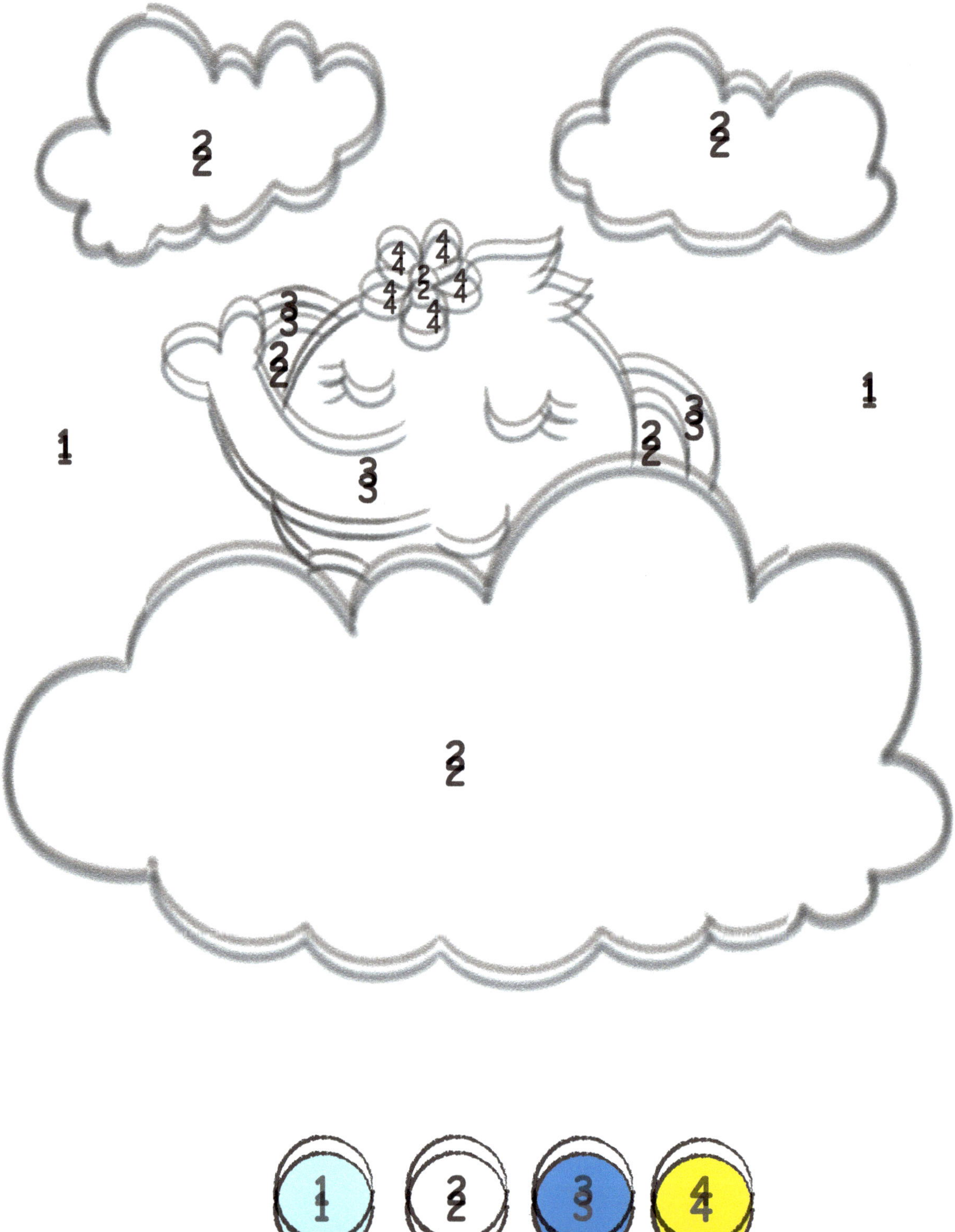

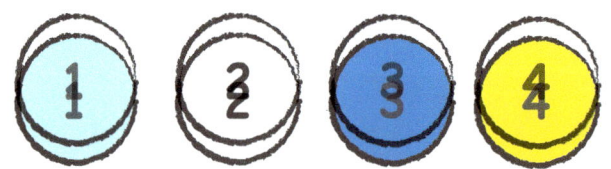

# Zoy's Fiery Frustration

# Zoy's Curious Quest

| 1 | 2 | 3 | 4 | 5 |

# Zoy's Loving Embrace

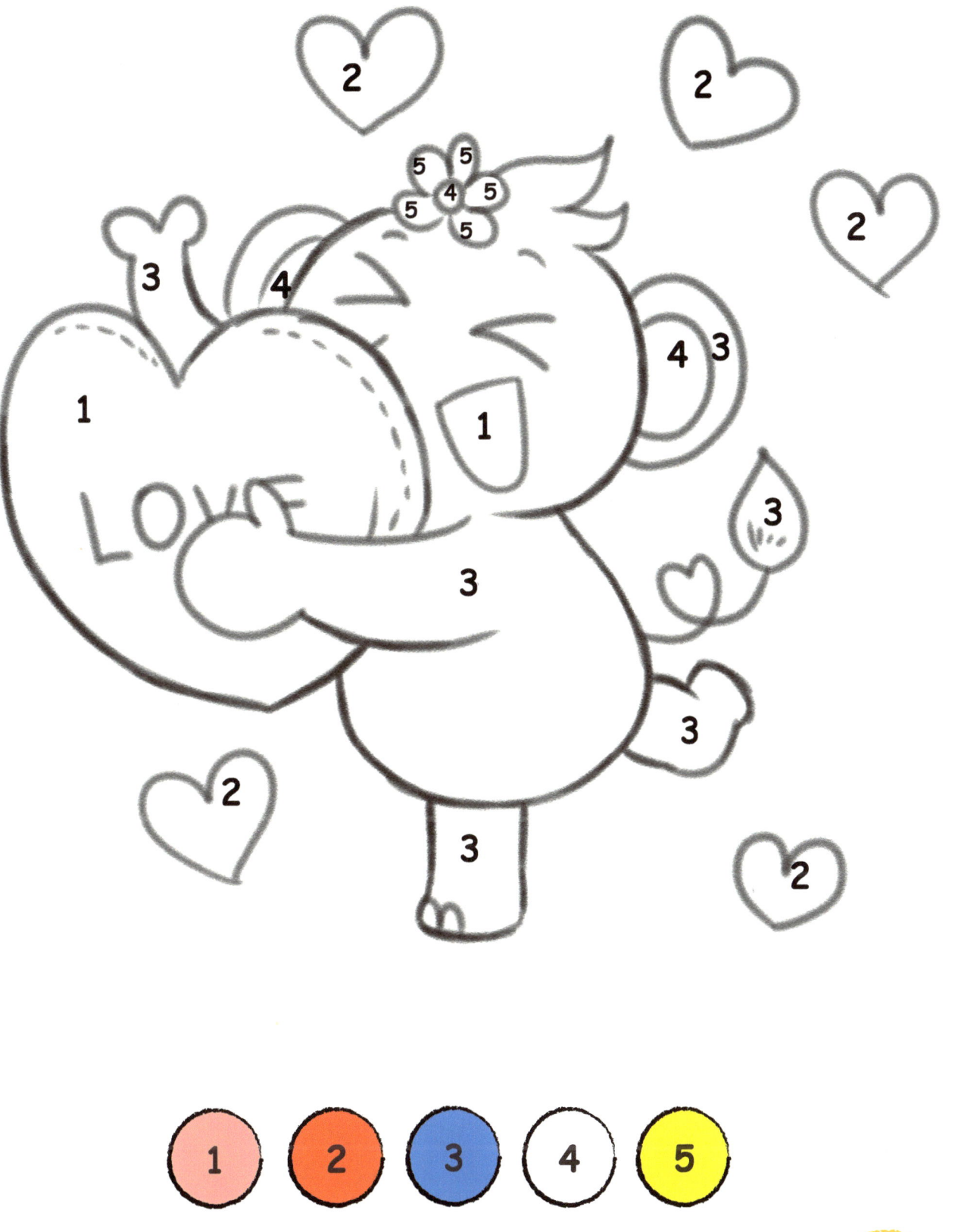

# Zoy's Fearful Freeze

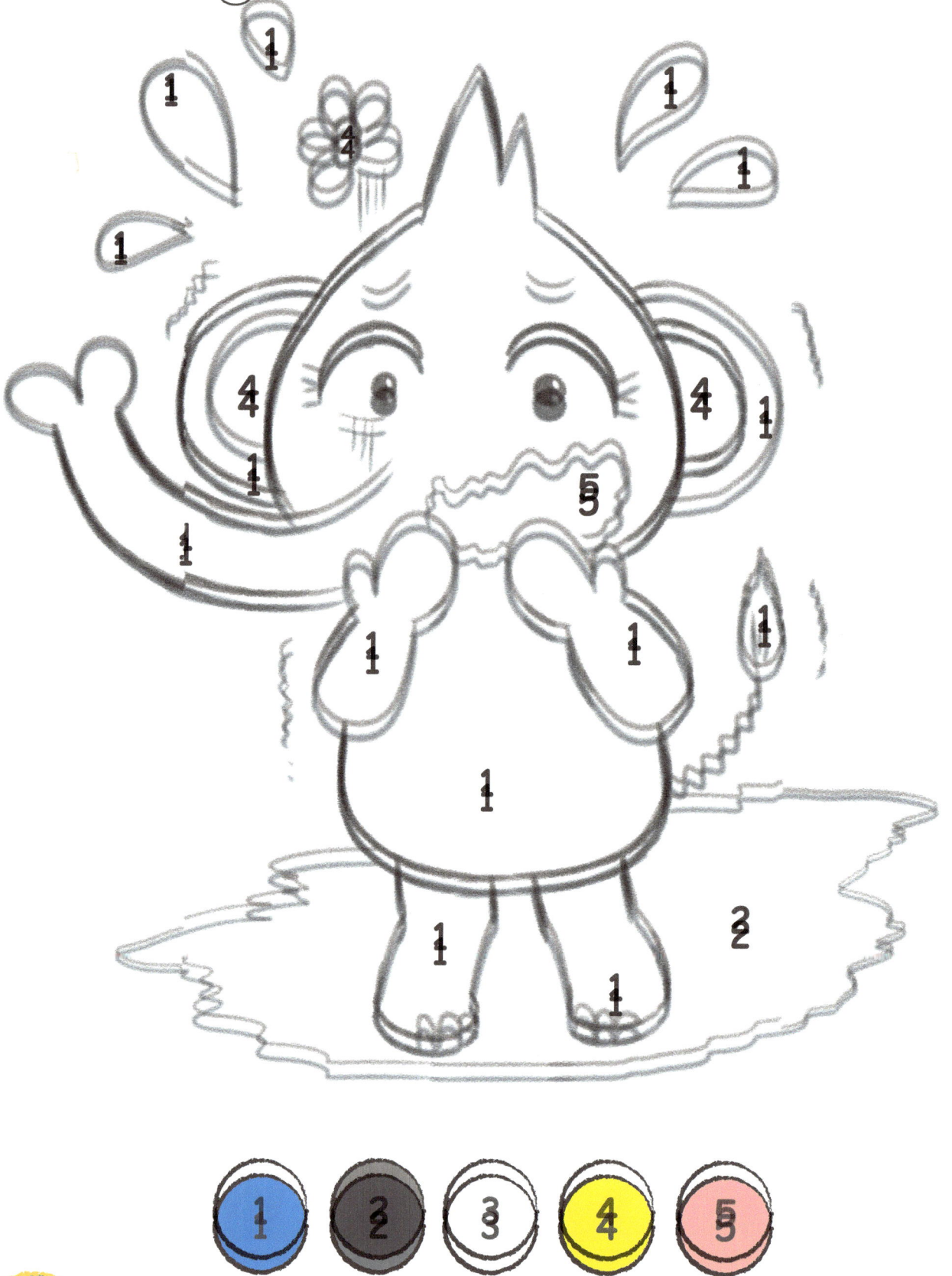

# Lil Ball's Patient Wait

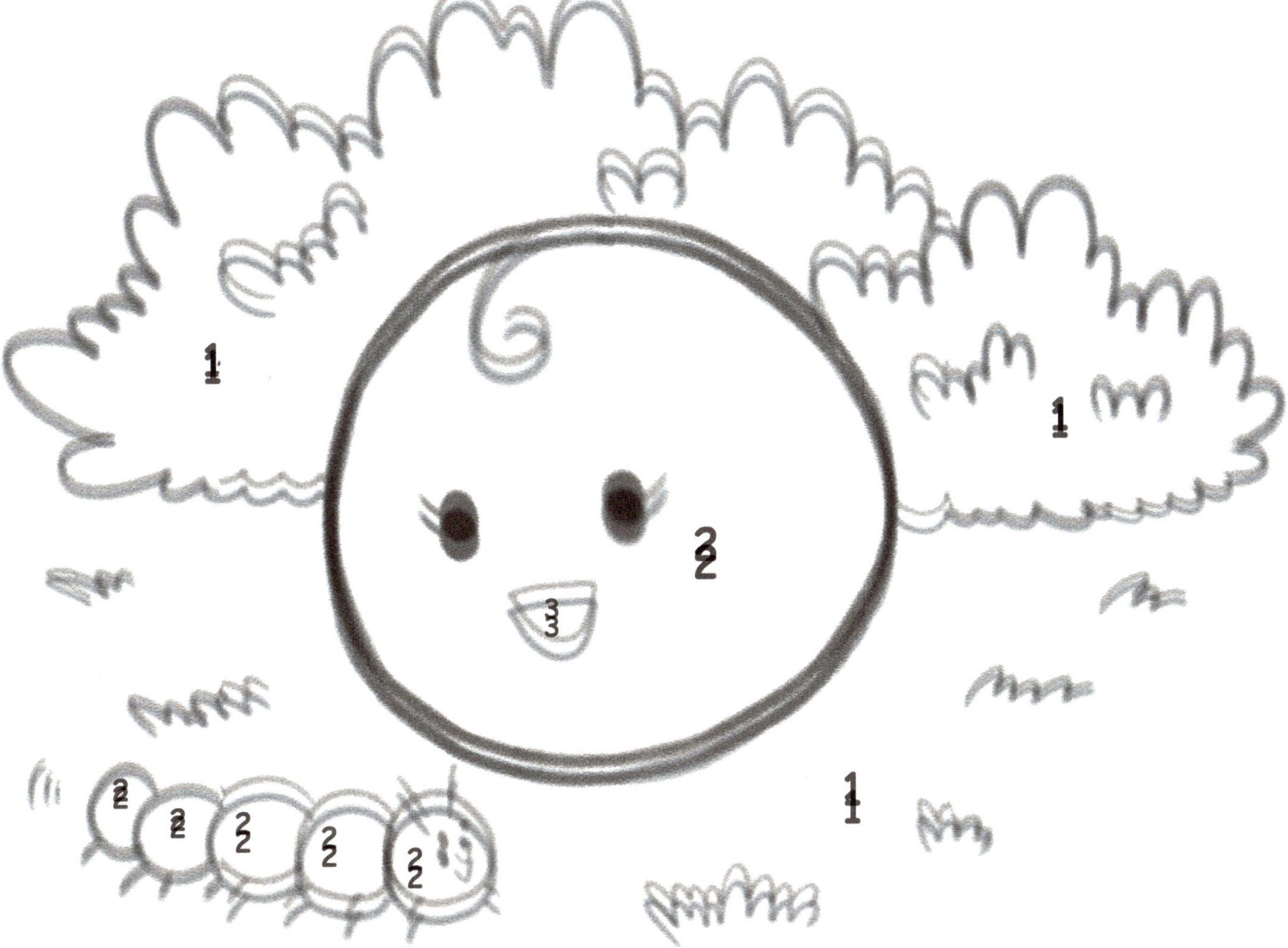

# Laughing Berries' Proud Stand

# Lil Ball's Trusting Tread

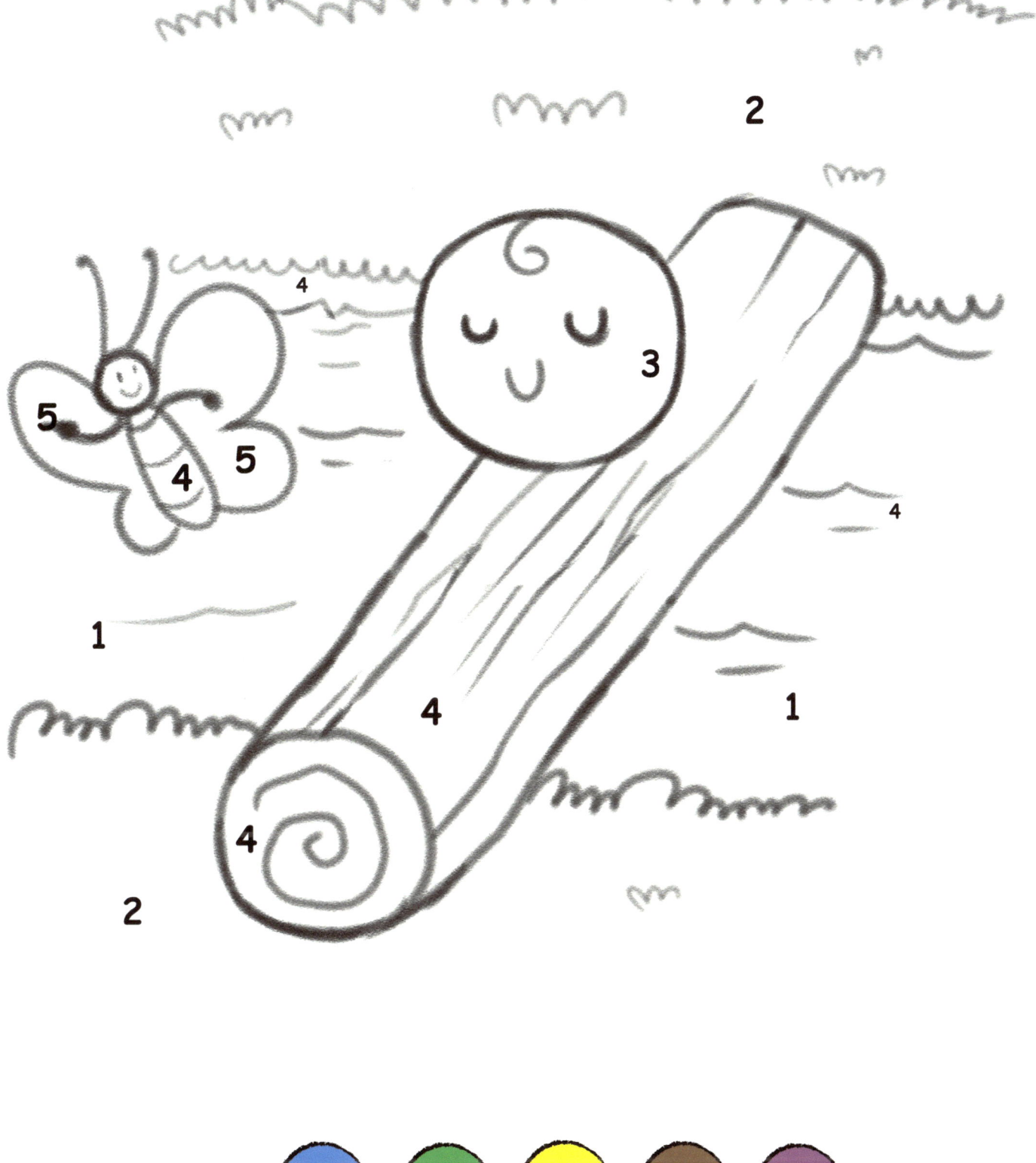

# Shyla's Hopeful Horizon

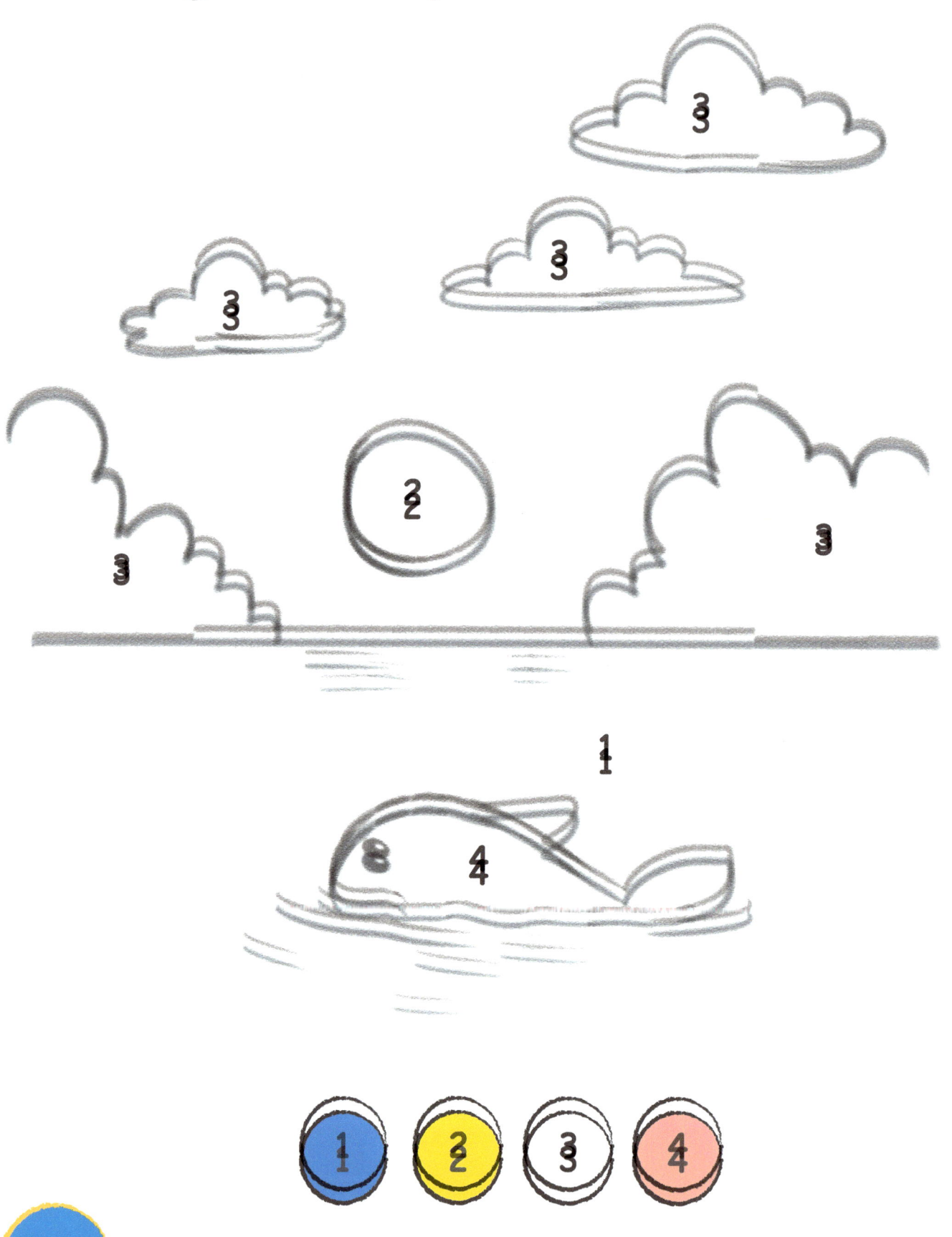

# Lil Ball's Disgusted Distance

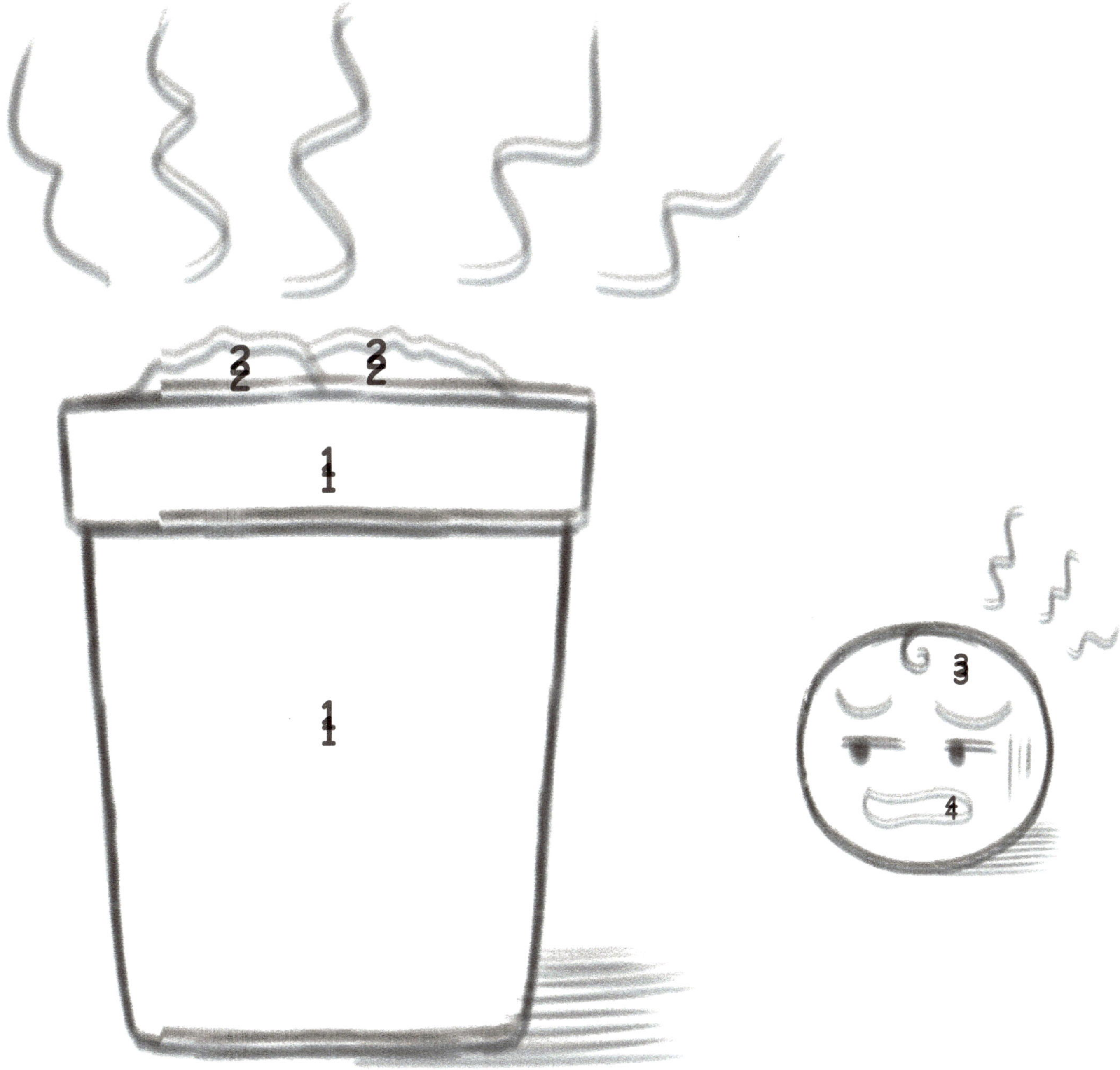

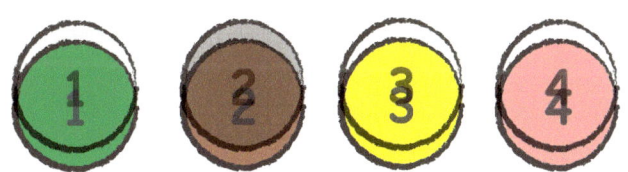

# Lil Ball's Envious Eye

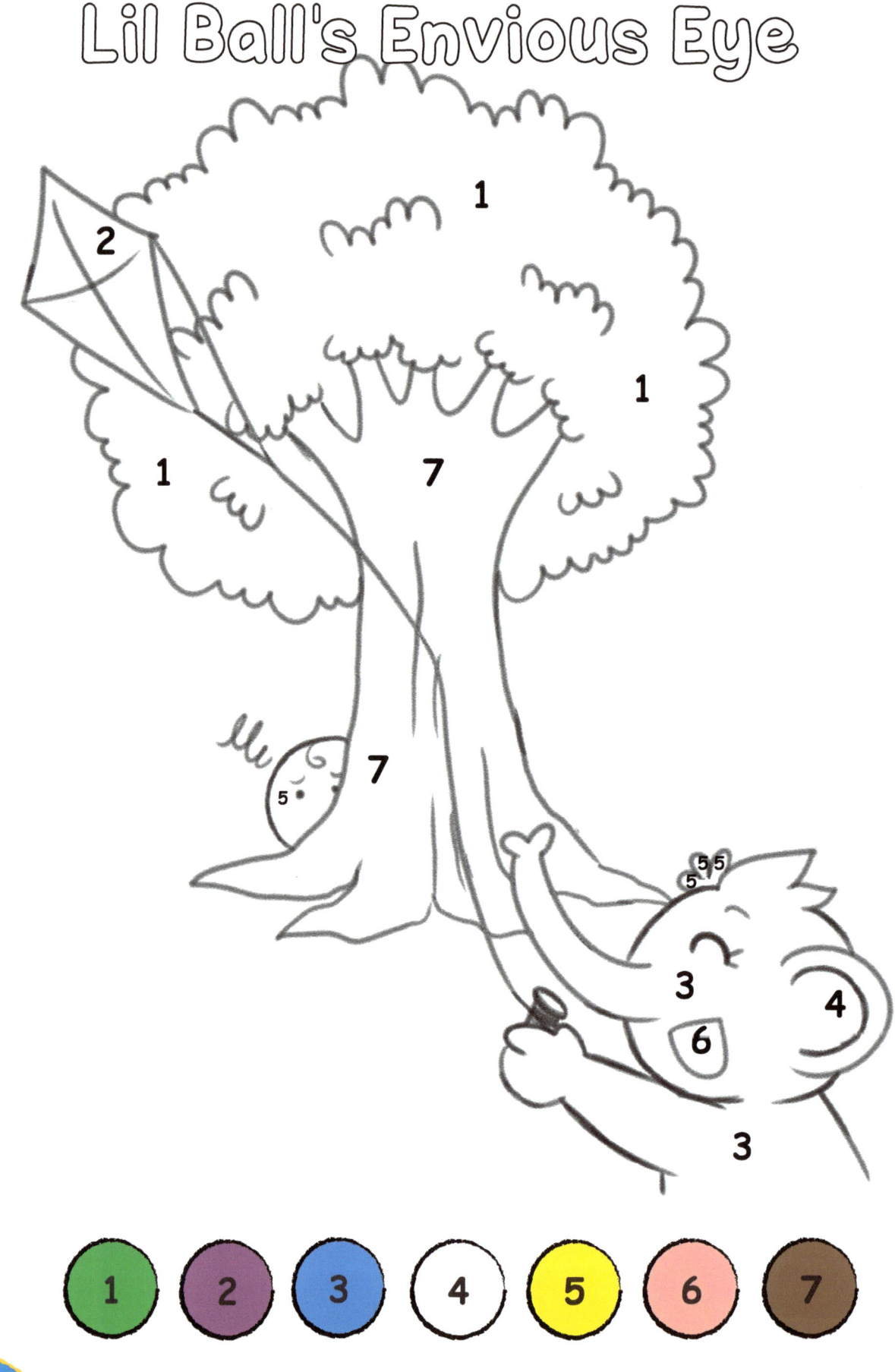

# Leigh's Surprised Sprout

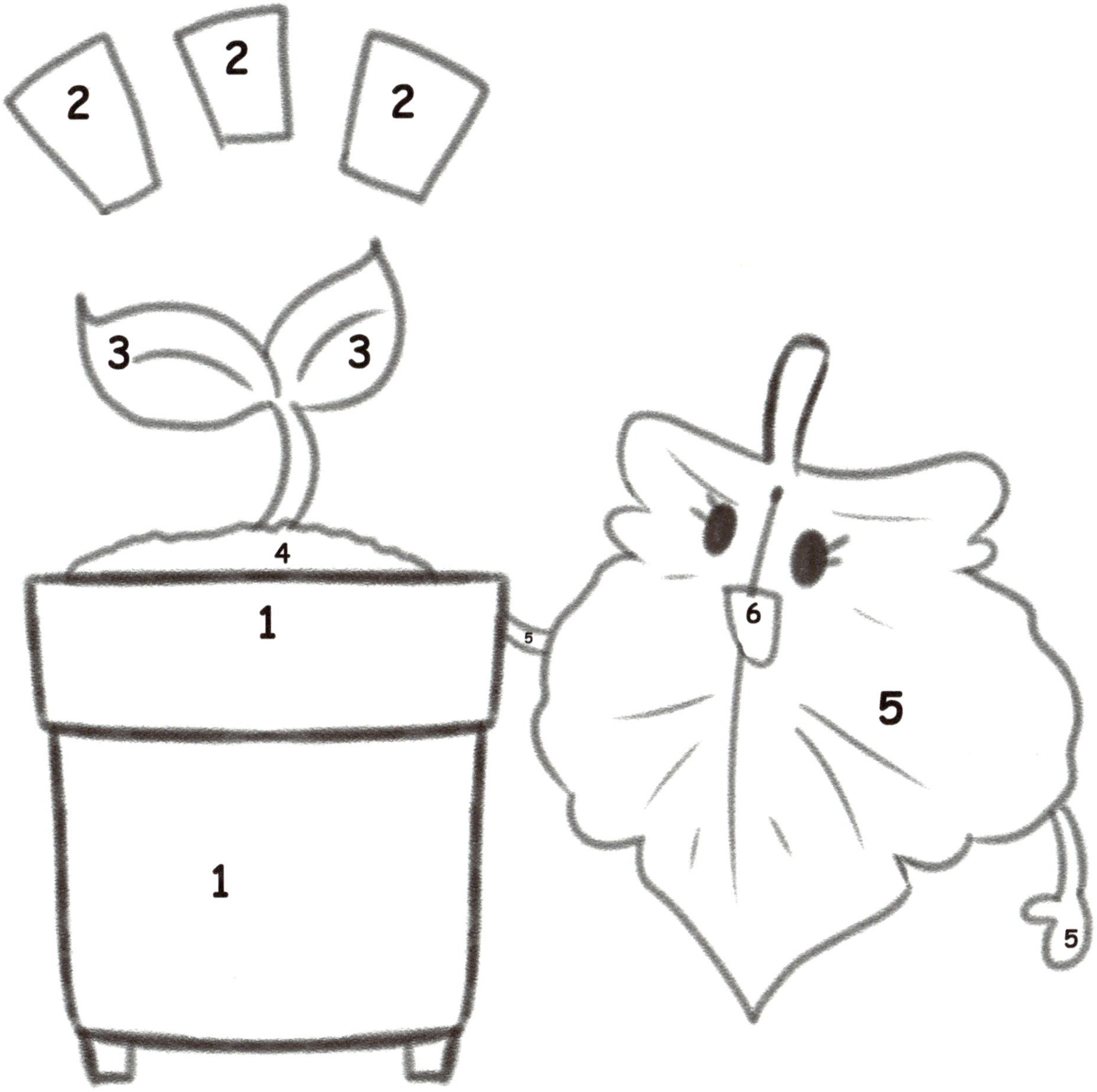

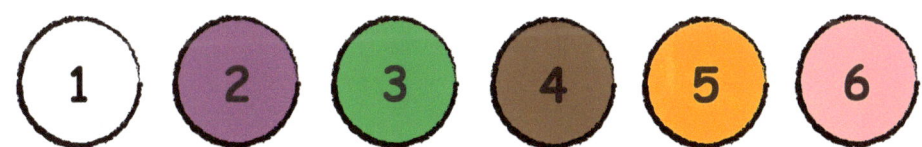

# Dogfish's Grateful Grin

# The Goofball's Brave Beam

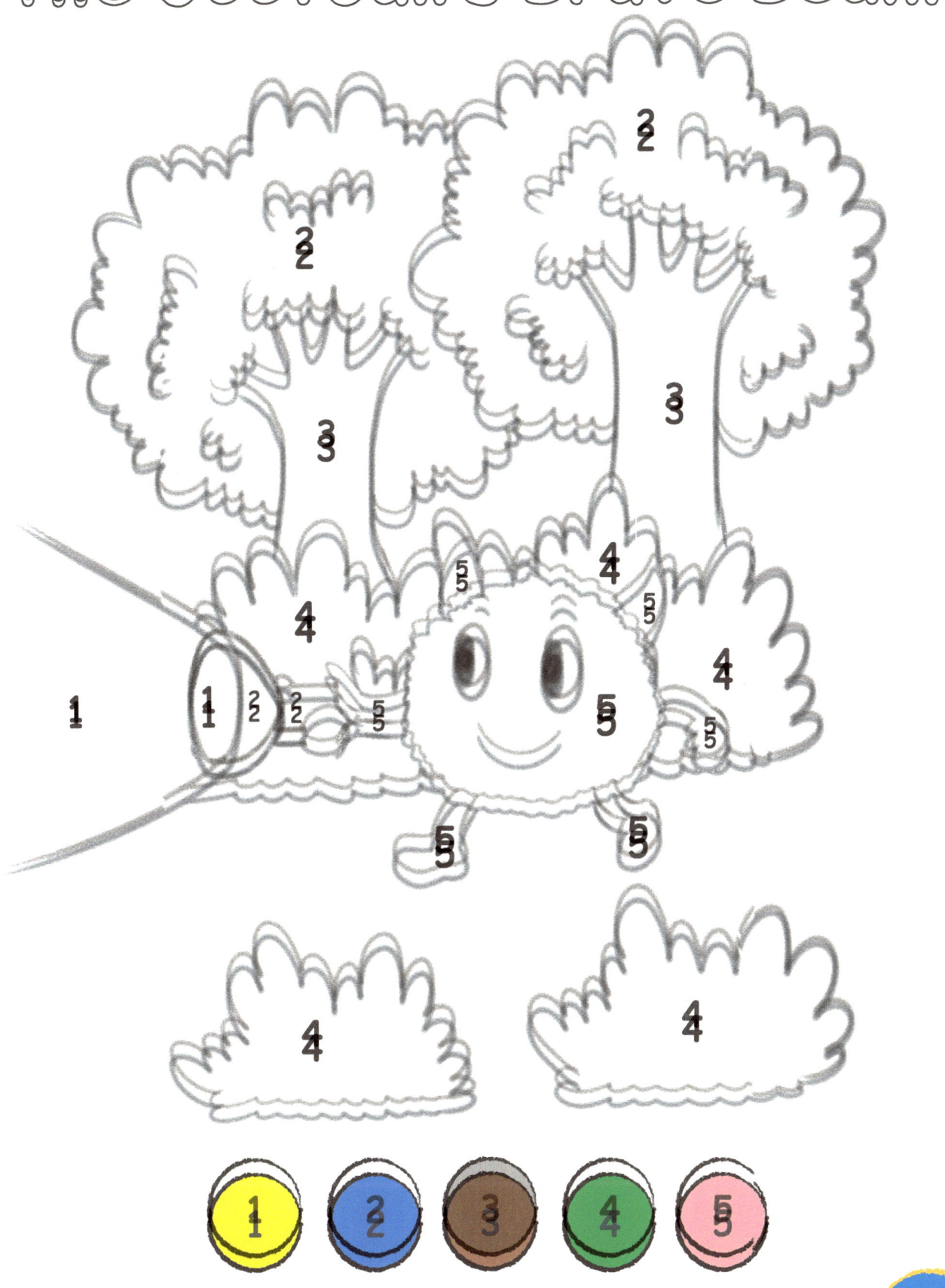

19

# The Goofball's Anticipating Awe

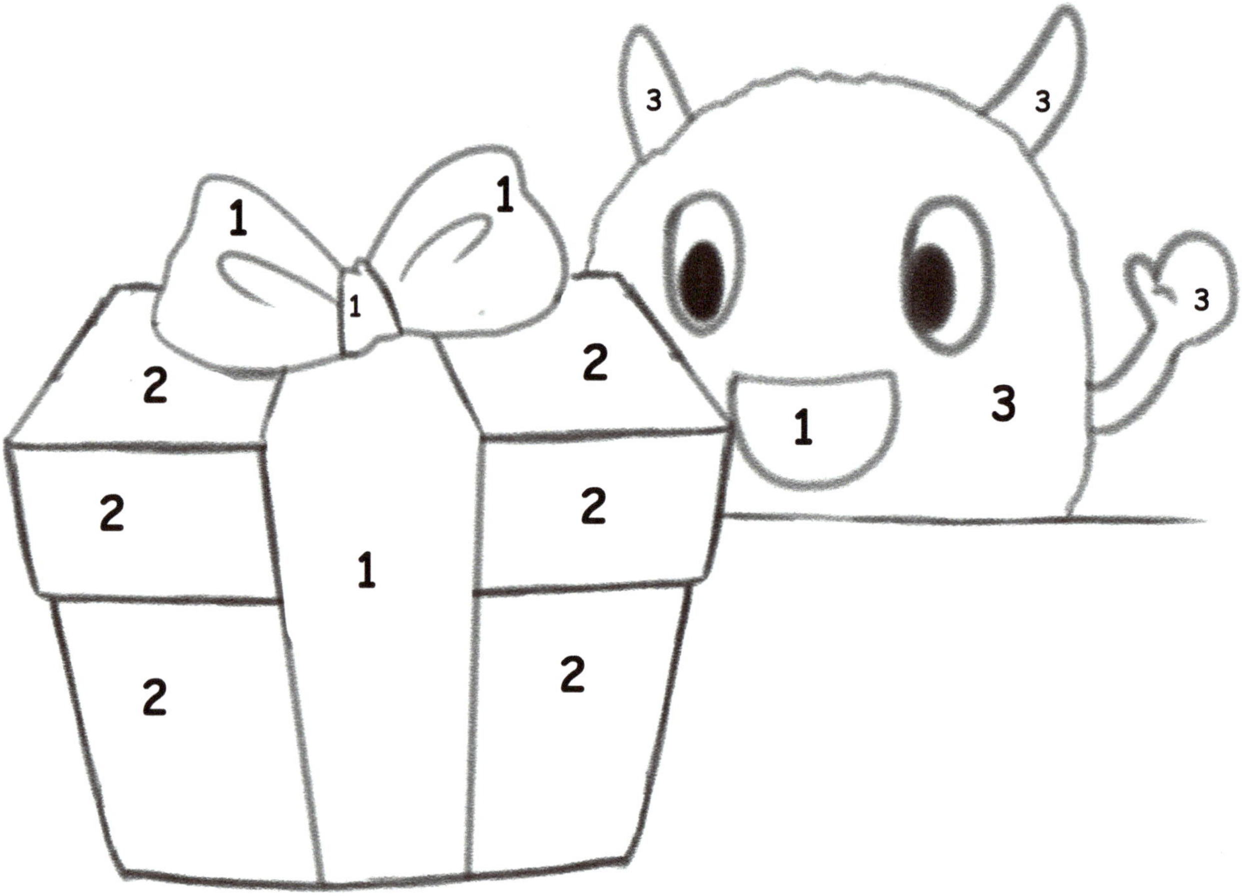

# Crab's Reflective Respite

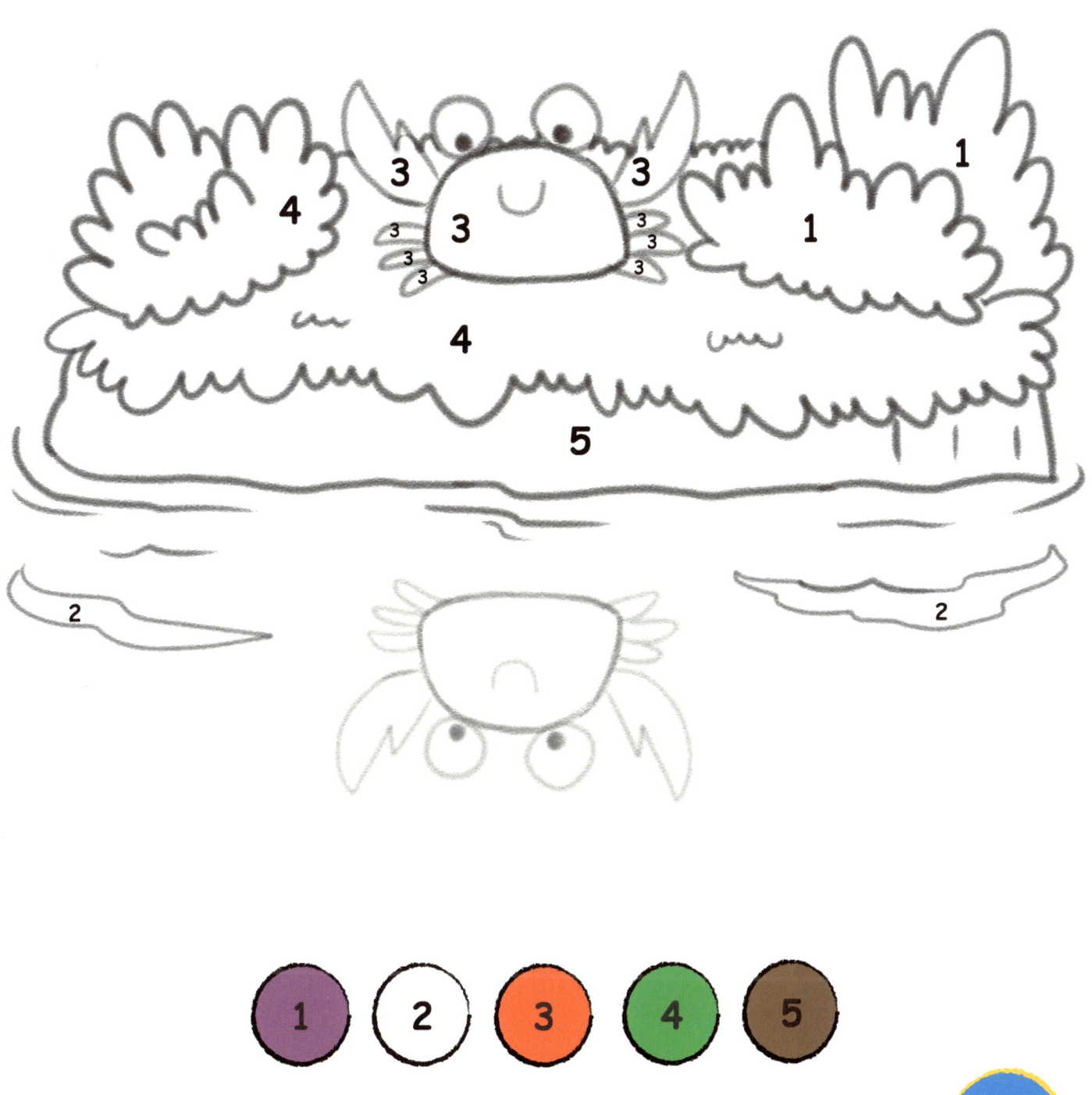

# Zoy's Contented Cuddle

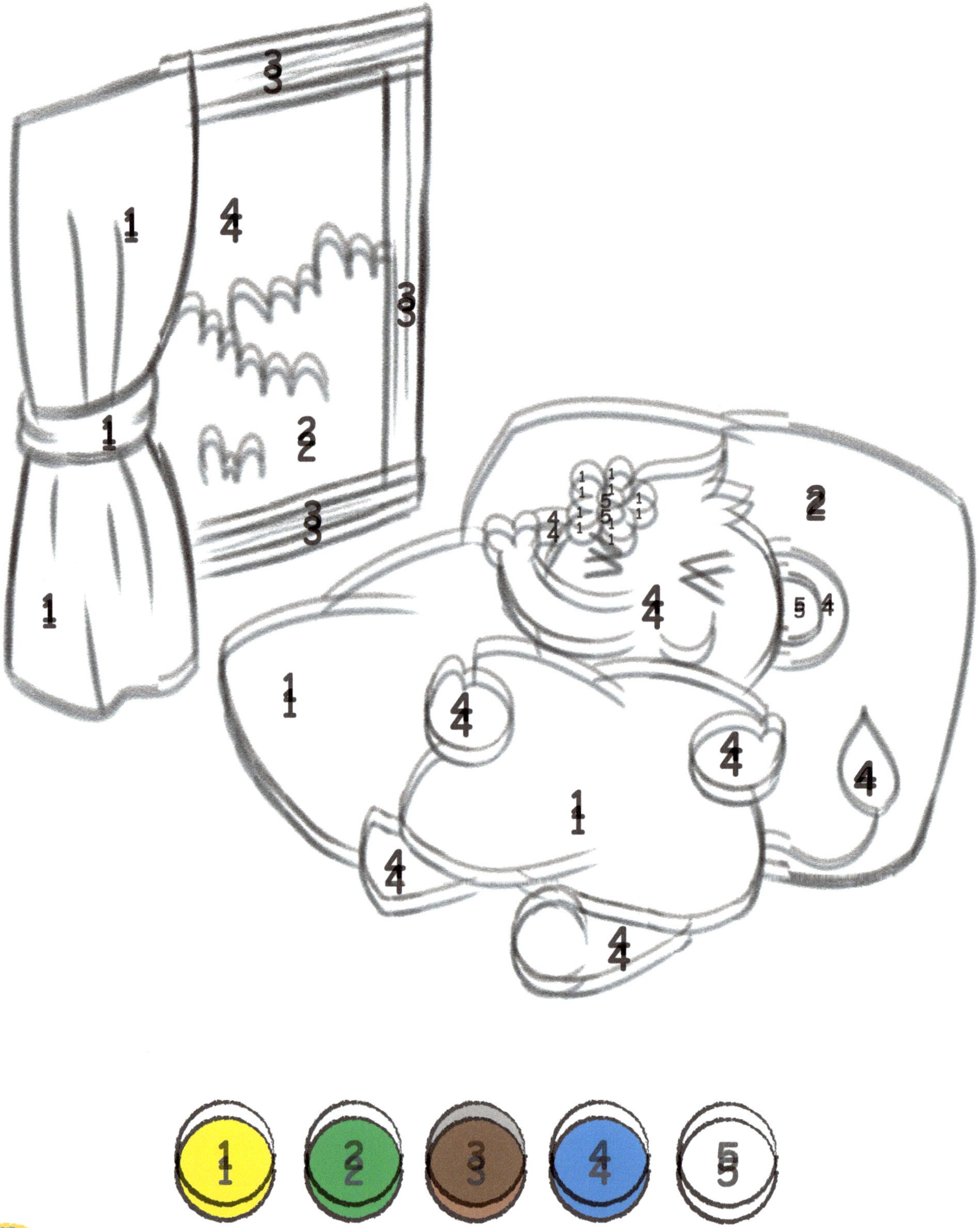

  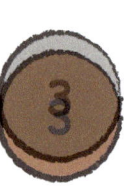  

# Lil Ball's Lonely Ledge

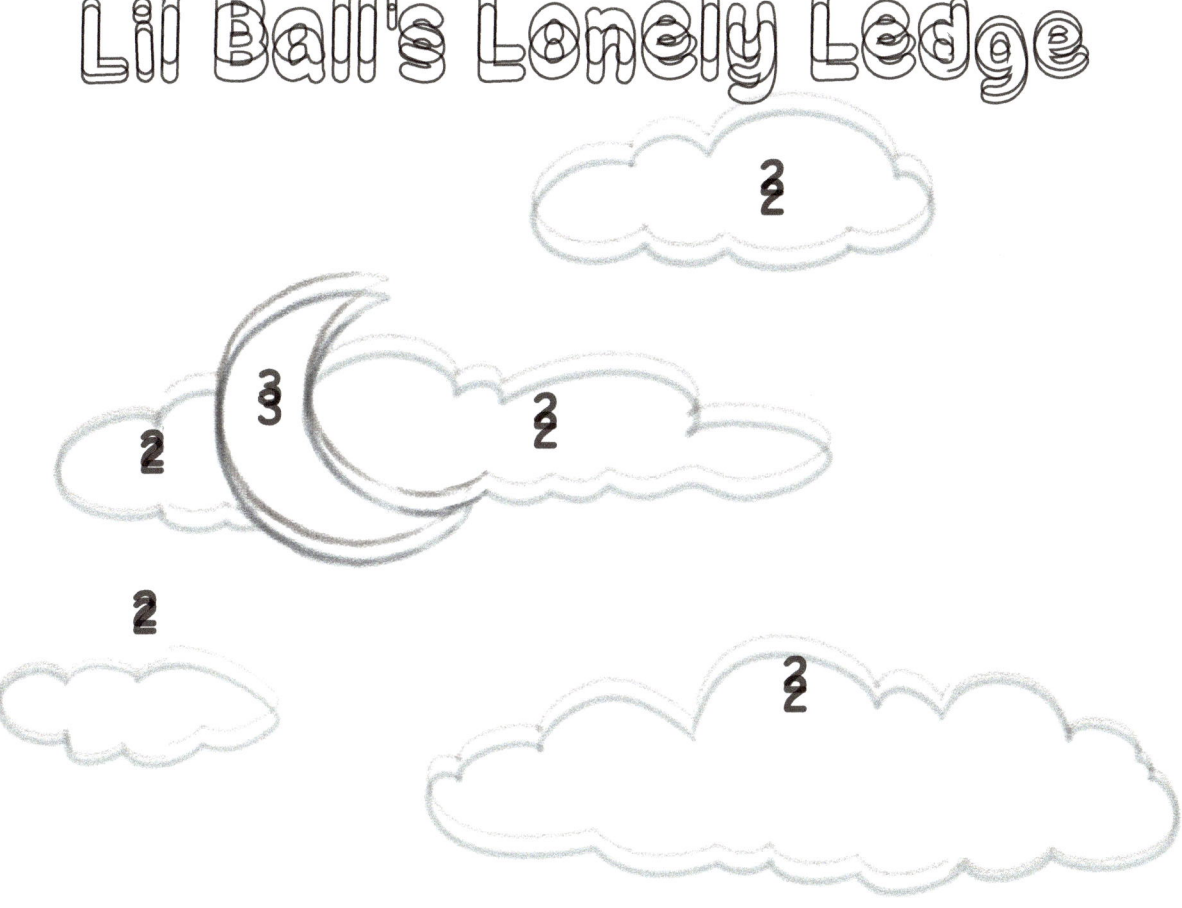
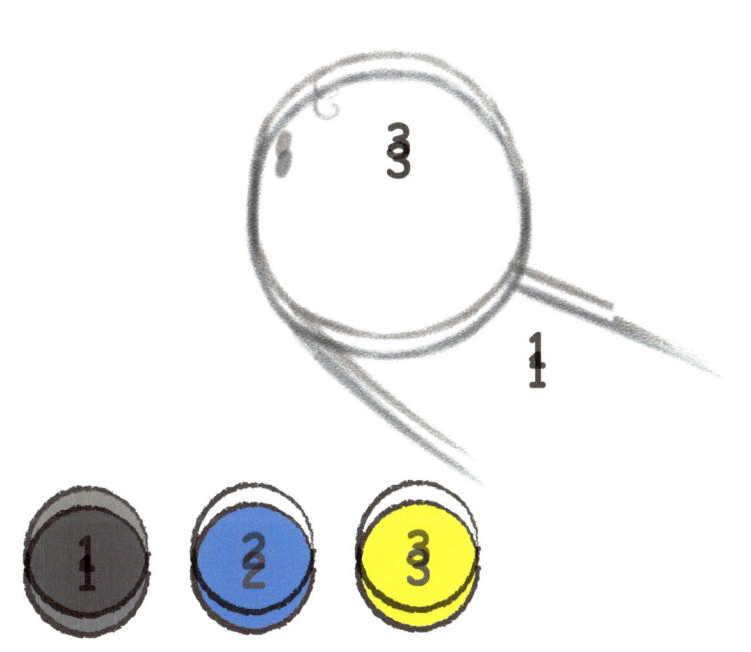

# Quincy's Amused Aplomb

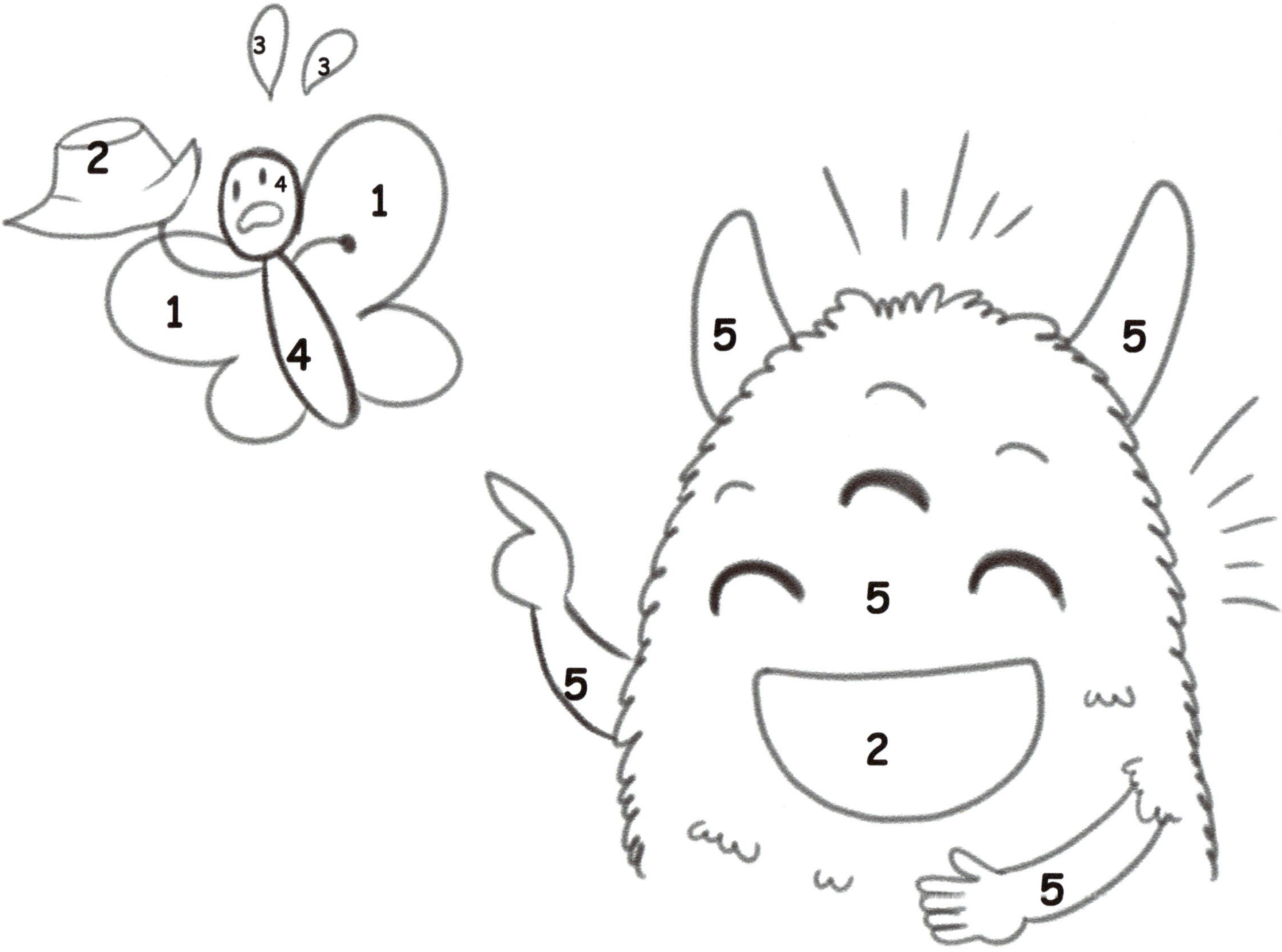

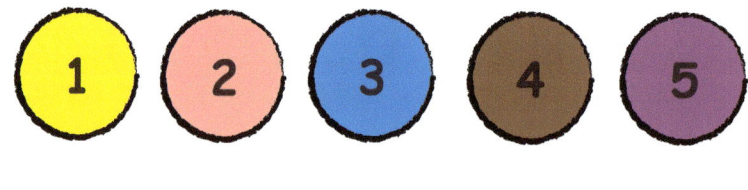

# Crab's Confident Climb

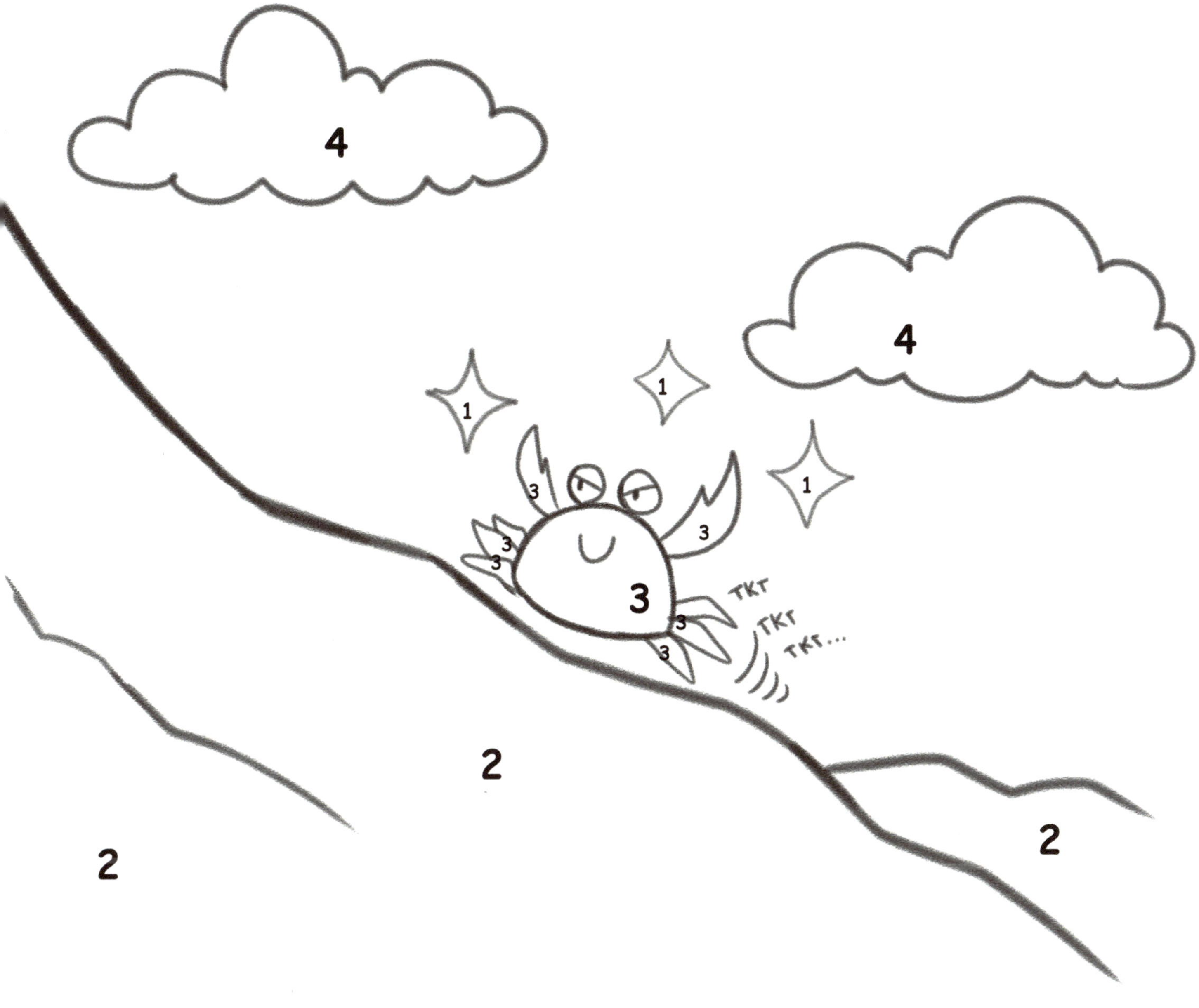

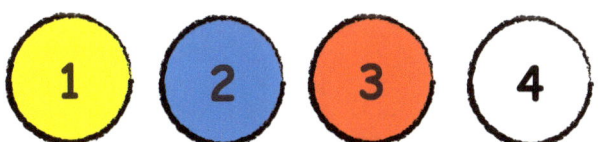

# The Hole's Humble Huddle

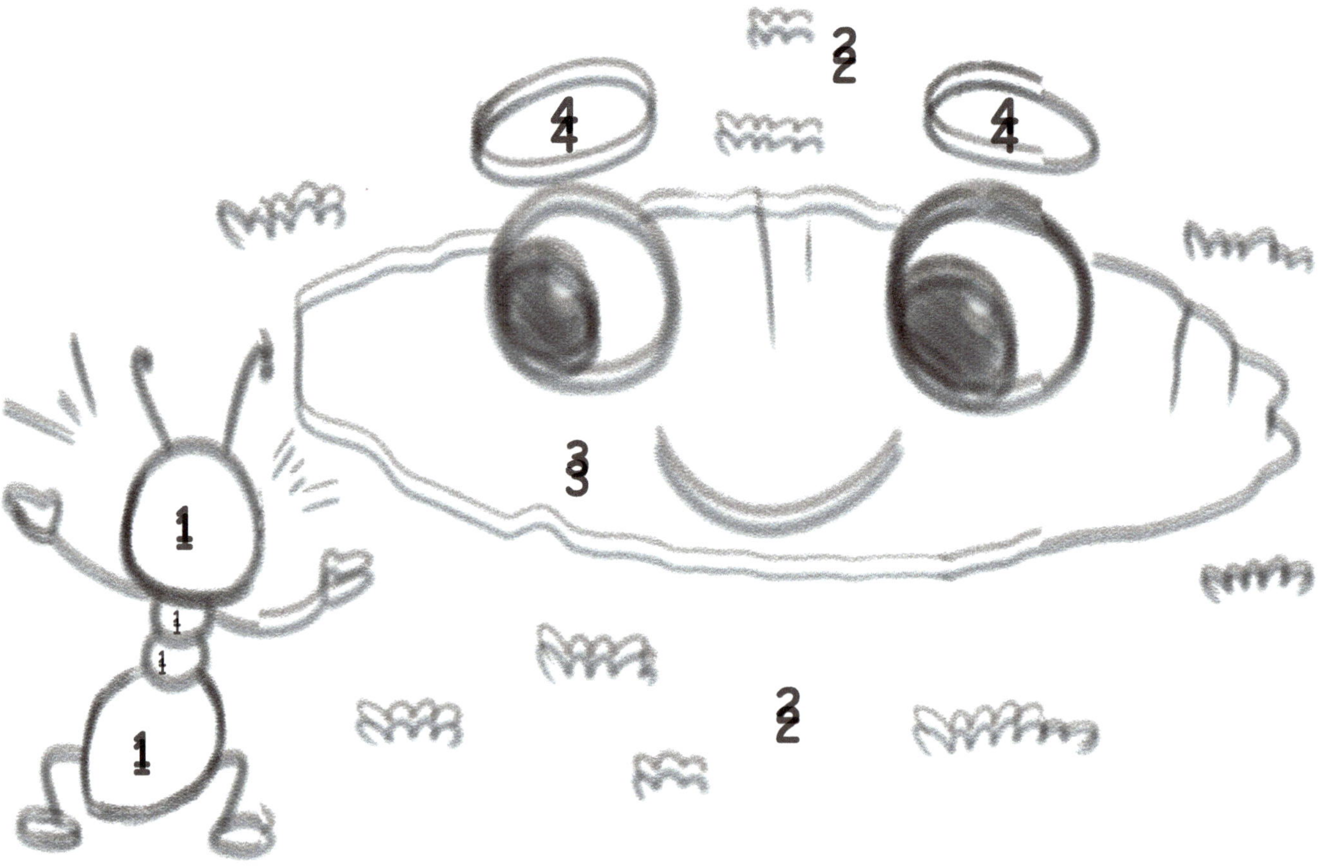

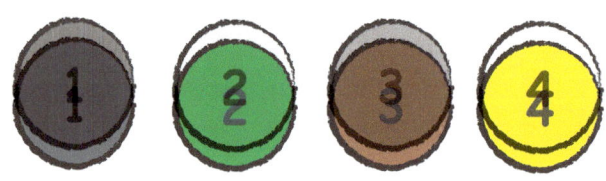

# Crab's Optimistic Outlook

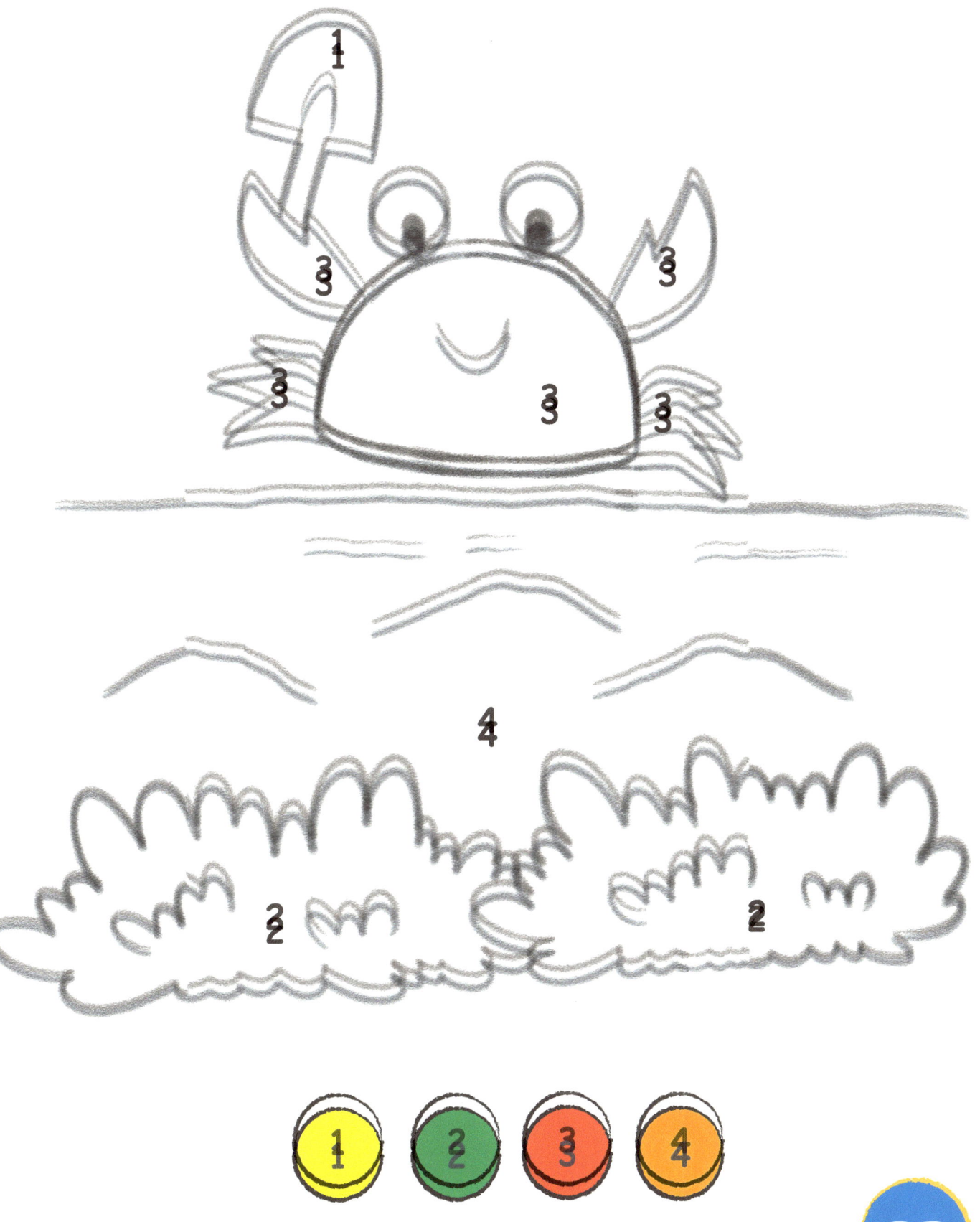

# Zoy's Friendship Fiesta

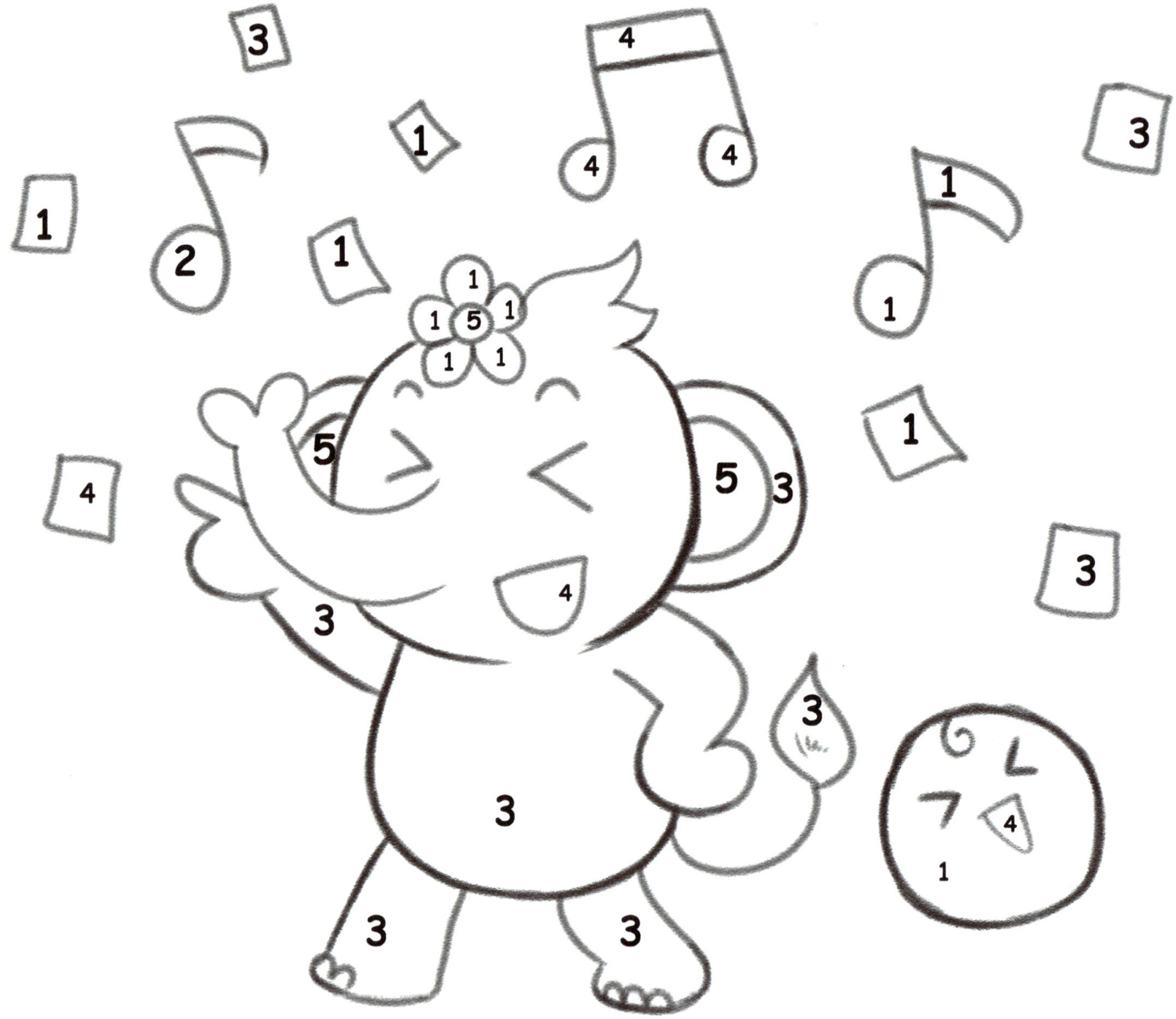

# Zoy's Sympathetic Sit-down

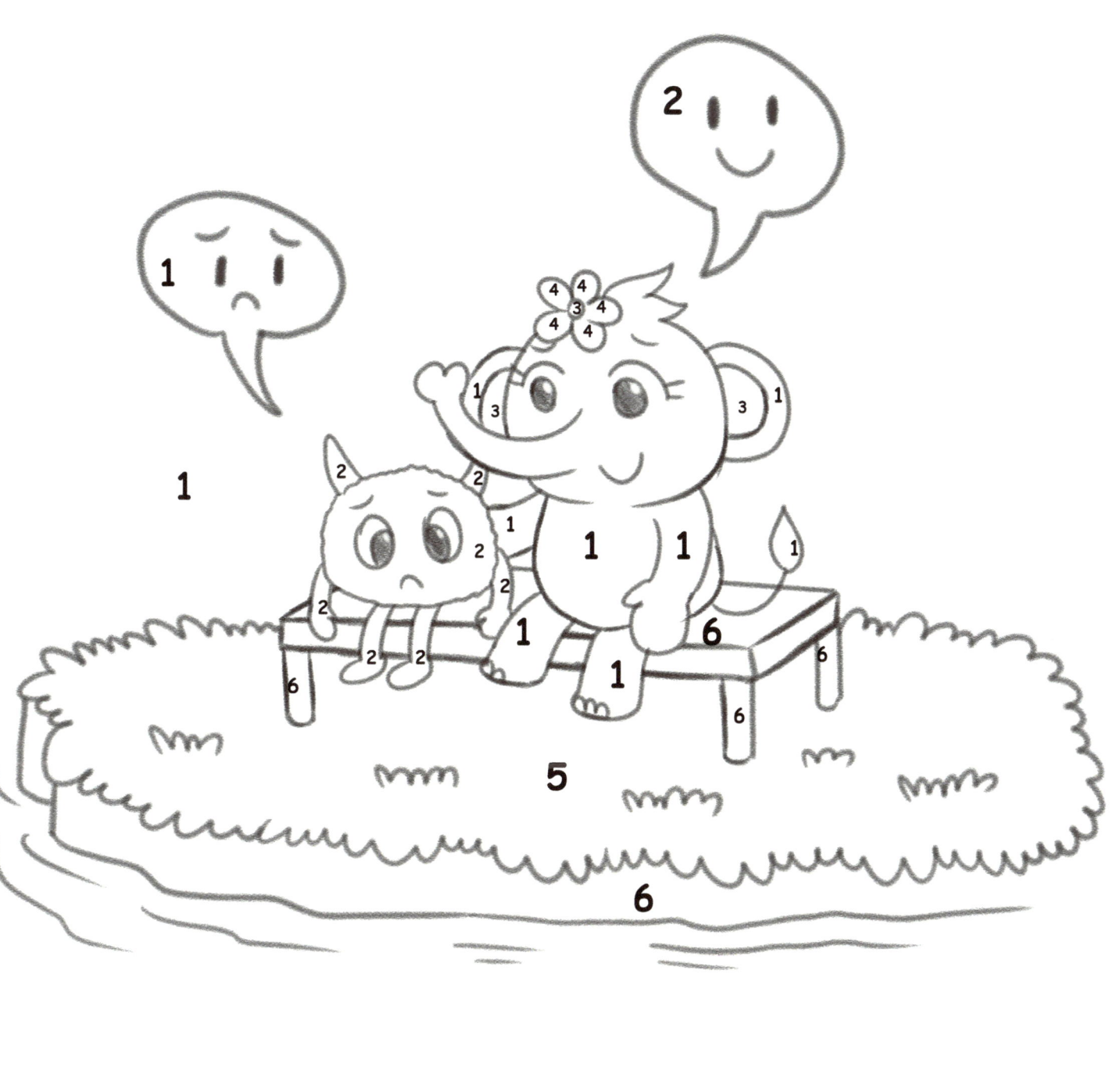

# Zoy's Team Triumph

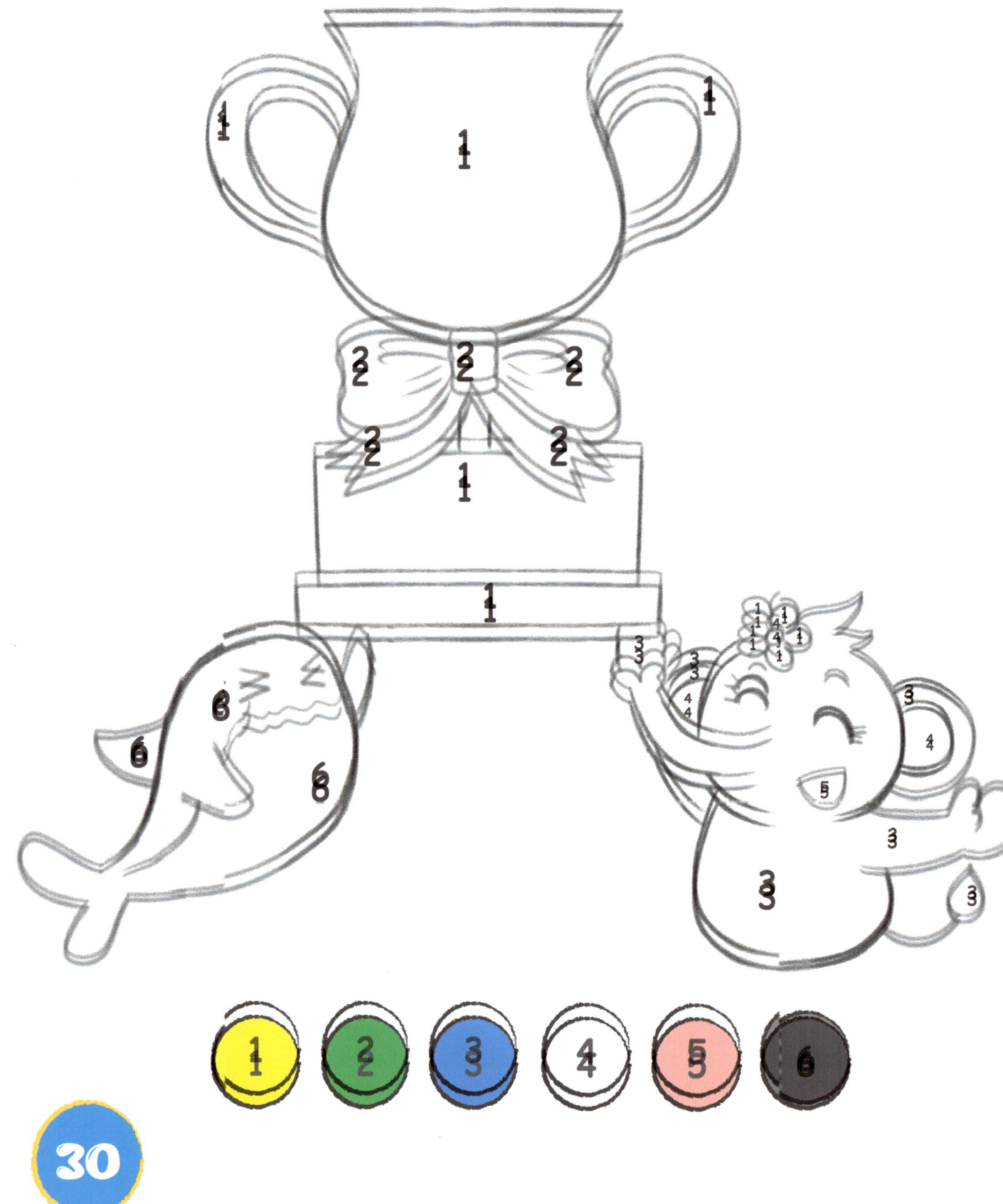

# Barry's Conflict & Resolution

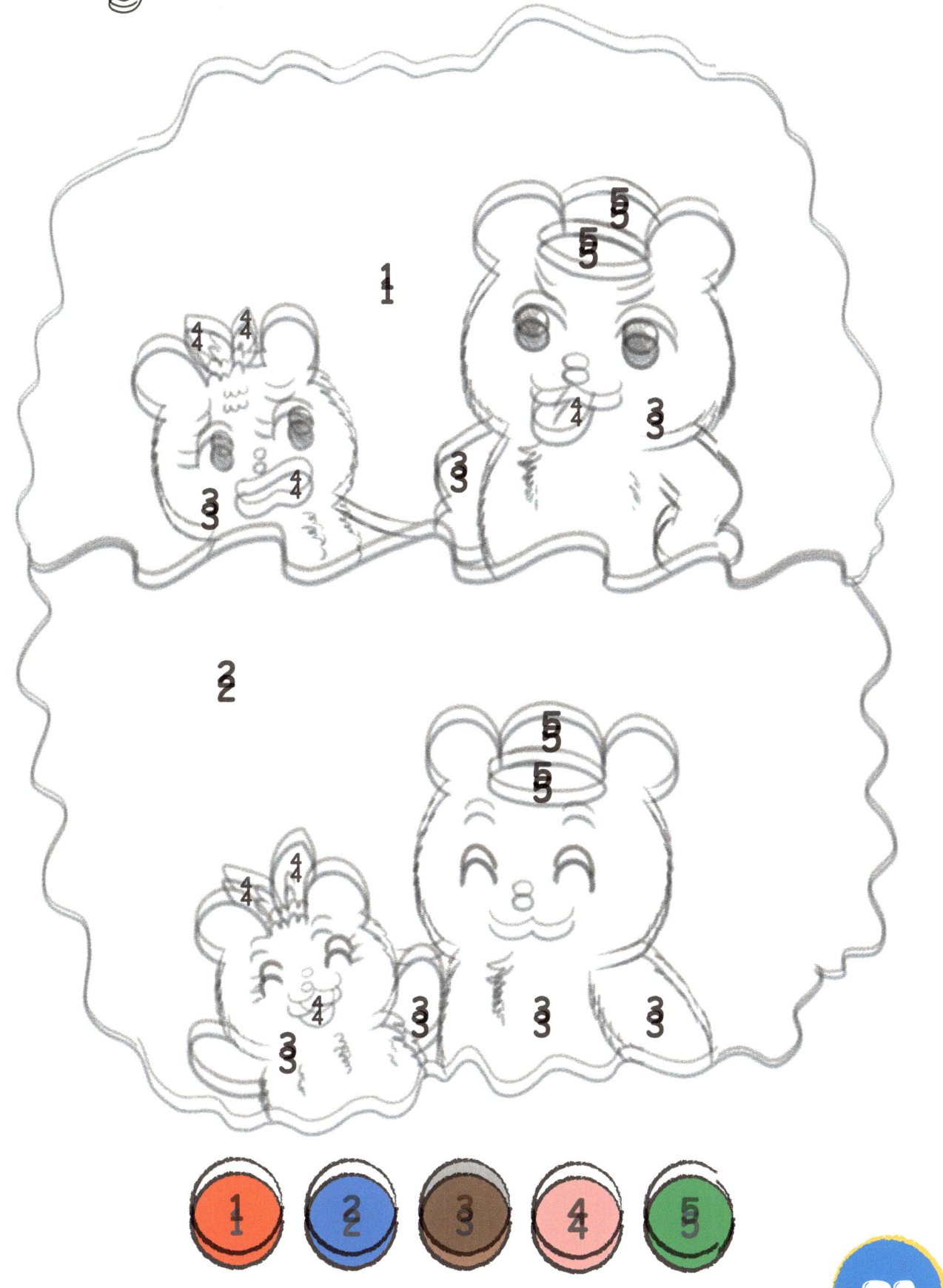

# Antony's Generous Give

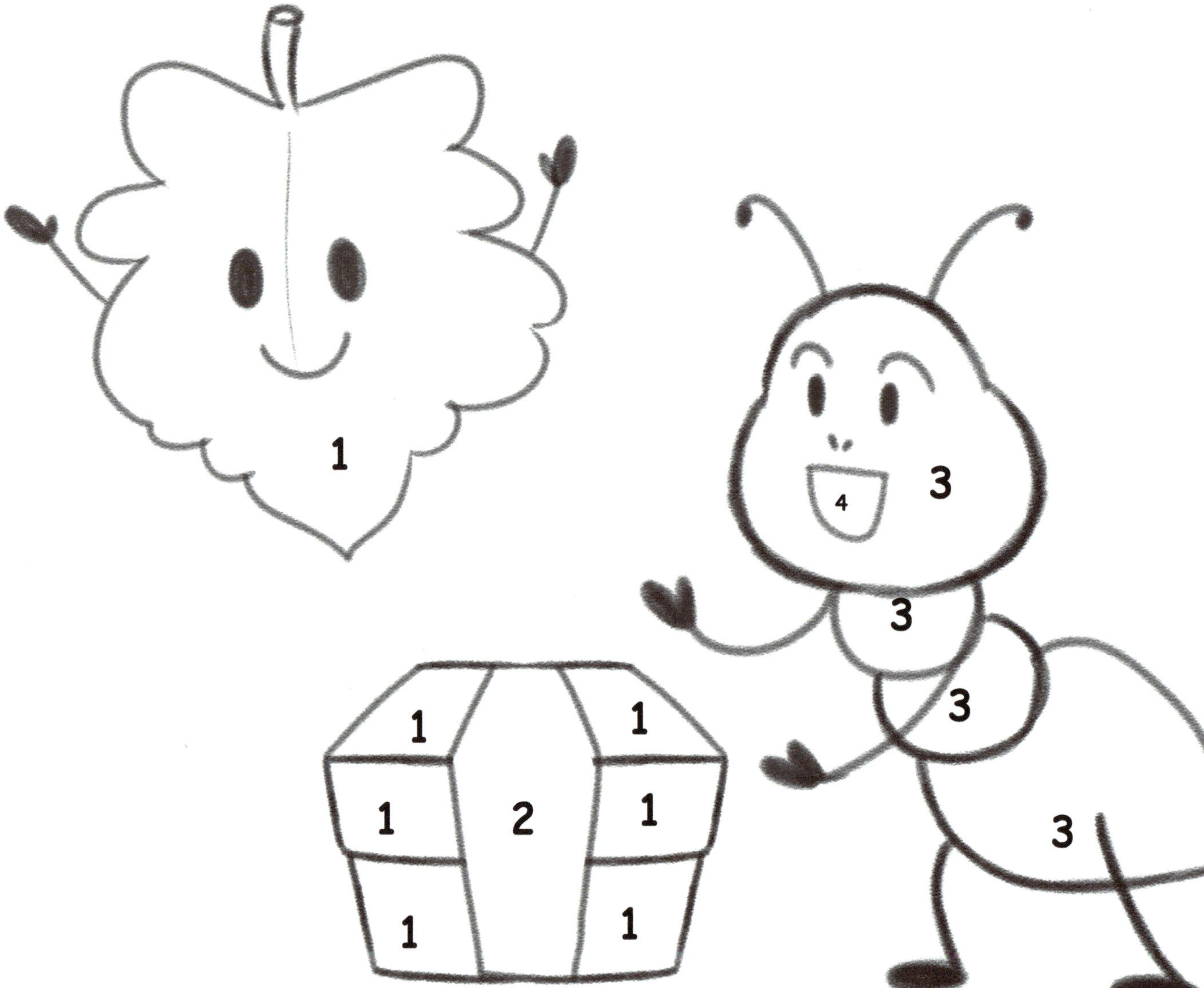

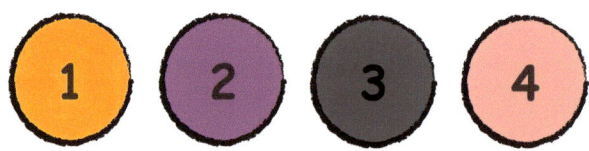

32

# Quincy's Tolerance Talk

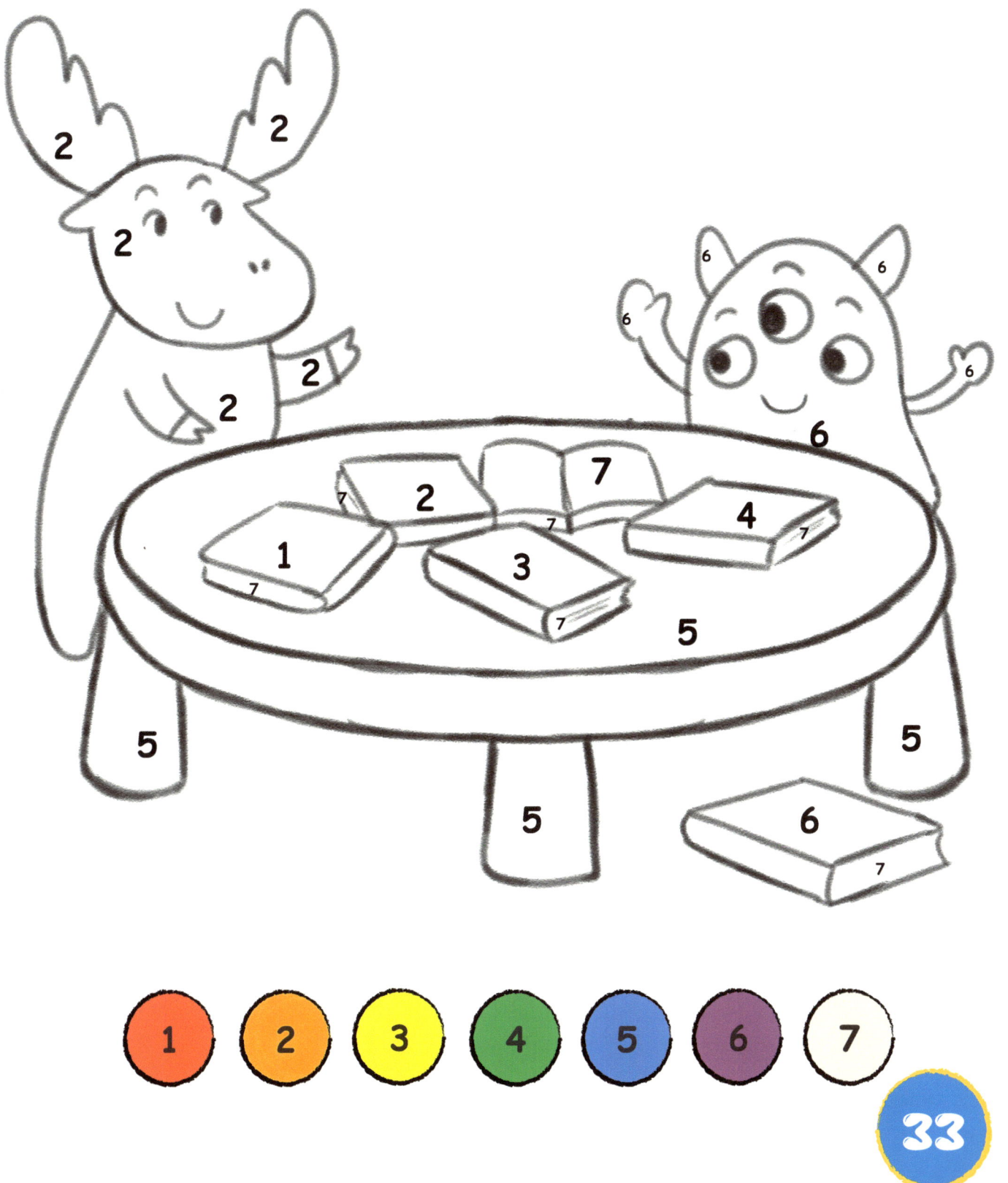

# Lil Ball's Respectful Rally

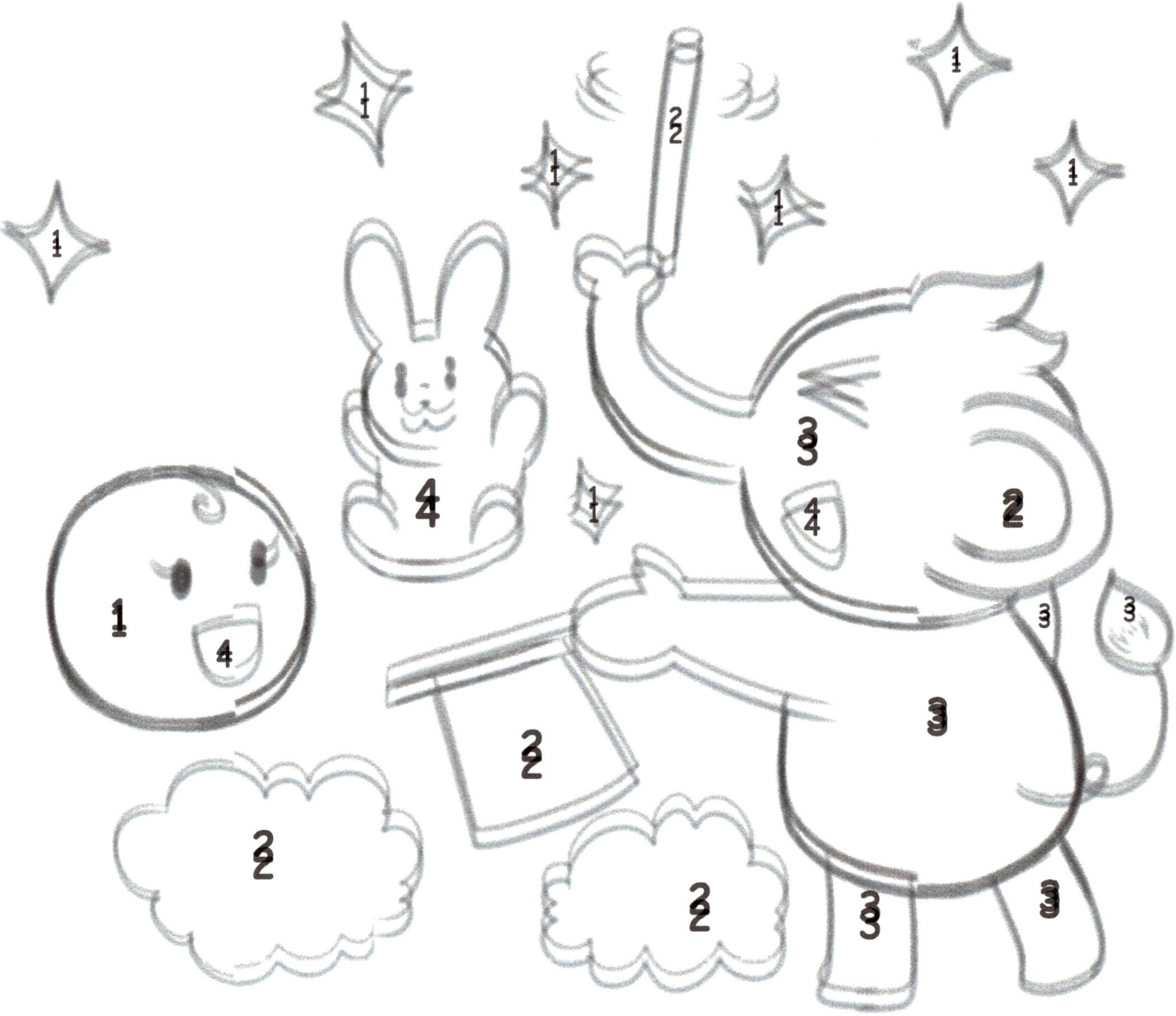

   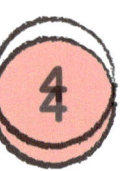

# Zoy's Compassionate Camp

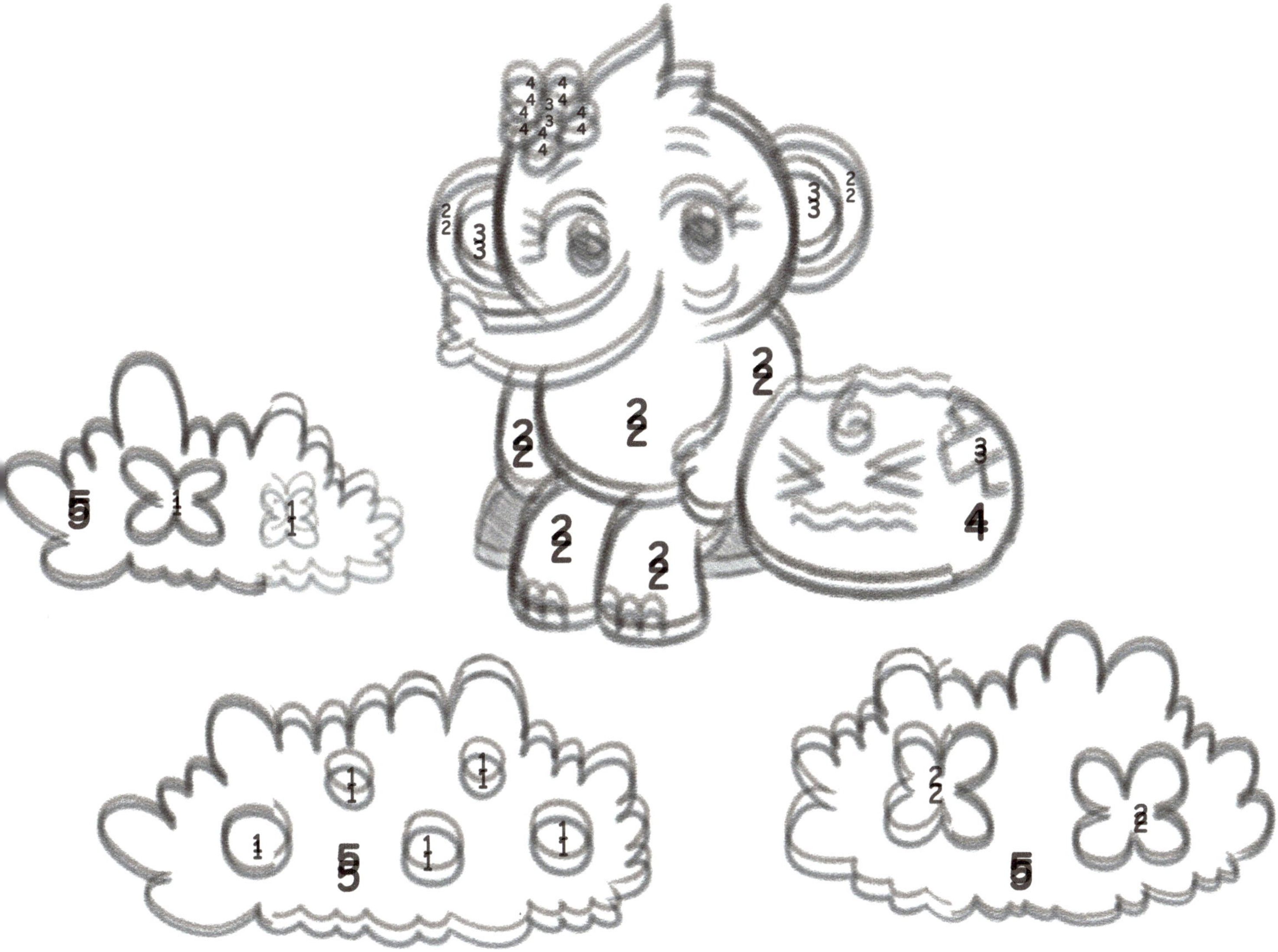

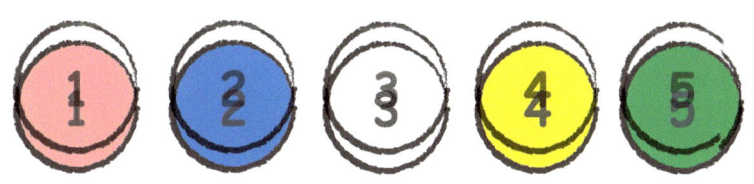

# Laughing Berries' Listening Lounge

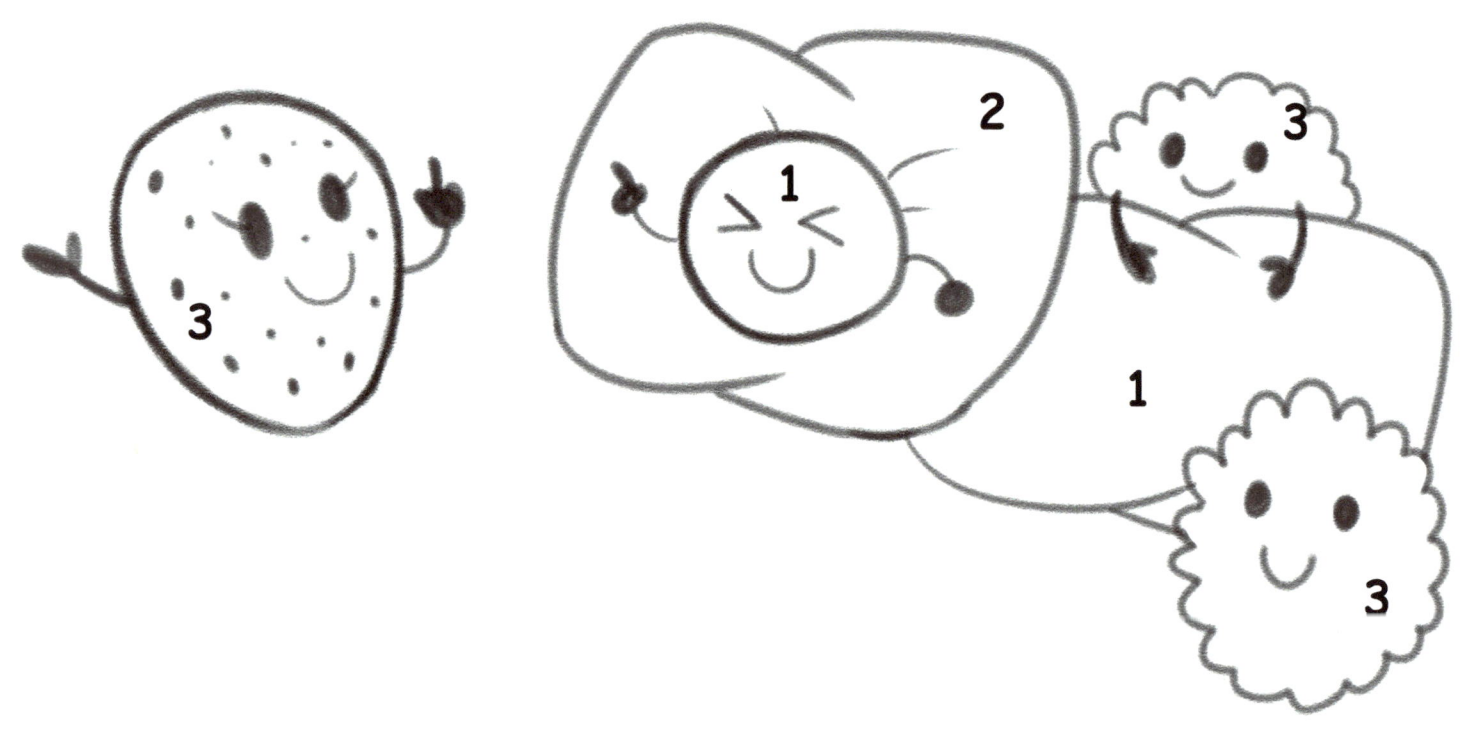

# Zoy's Honesty Hour

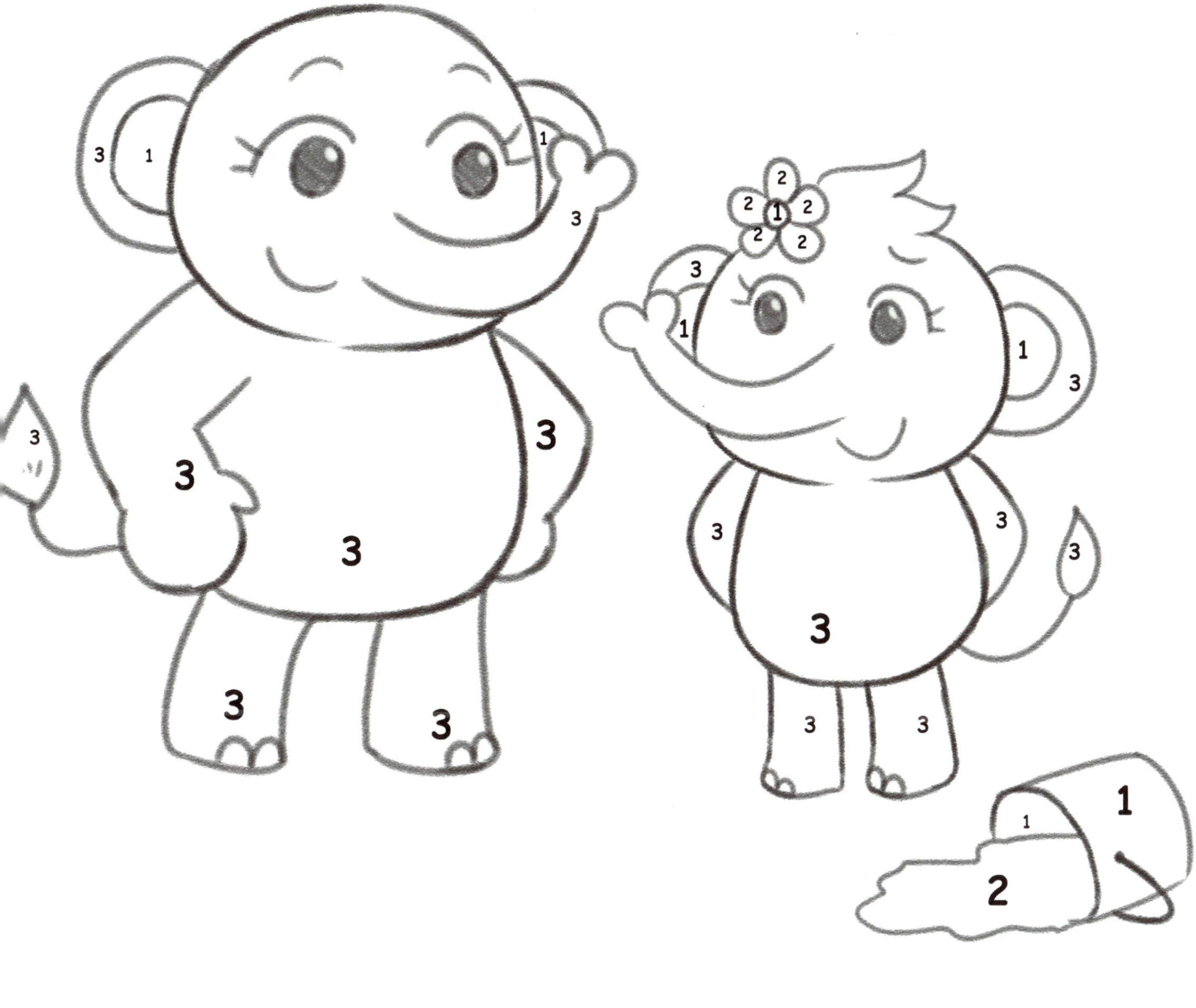

# Zoy's Playful Parade

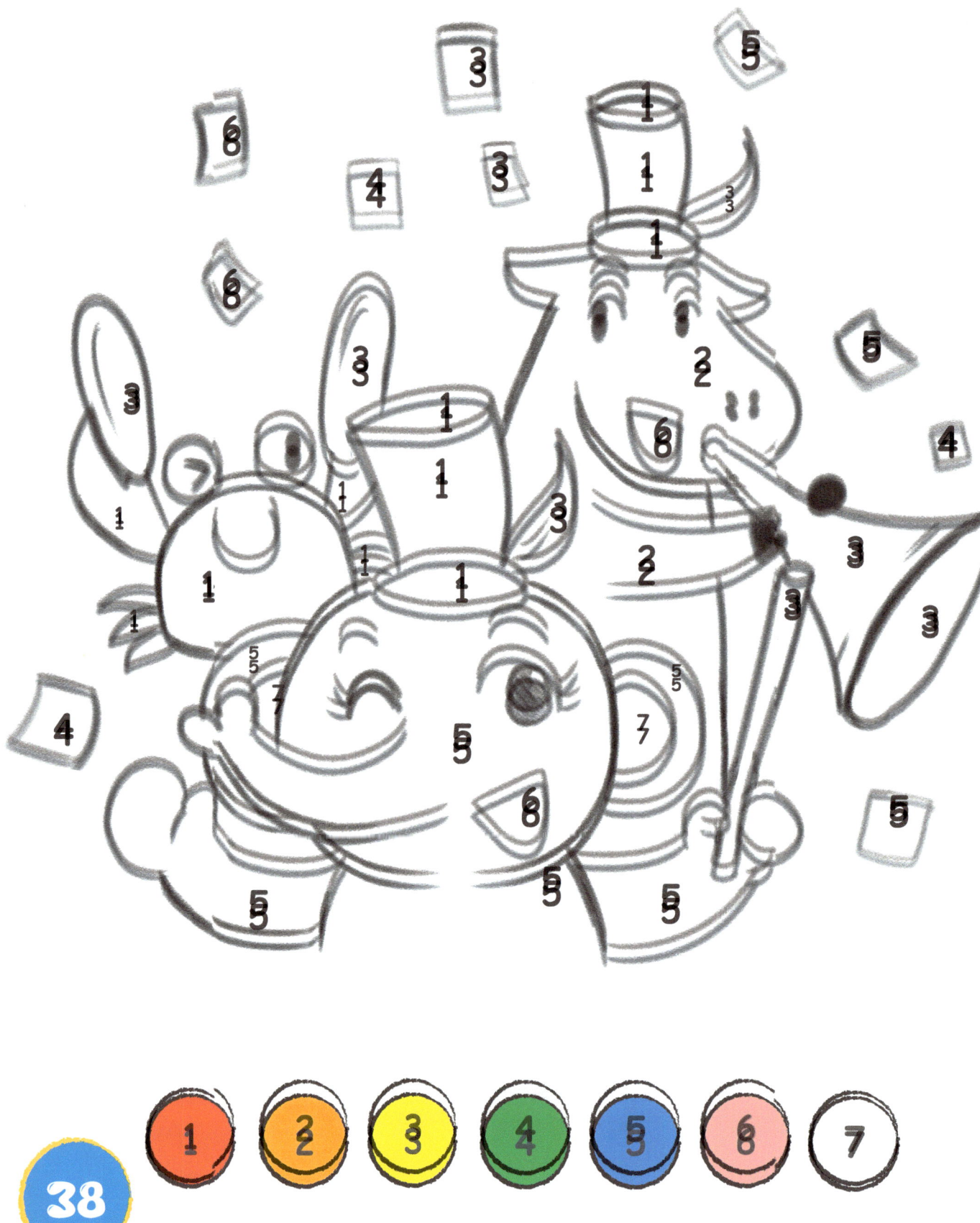

# The Goofball's Forgiving Forest

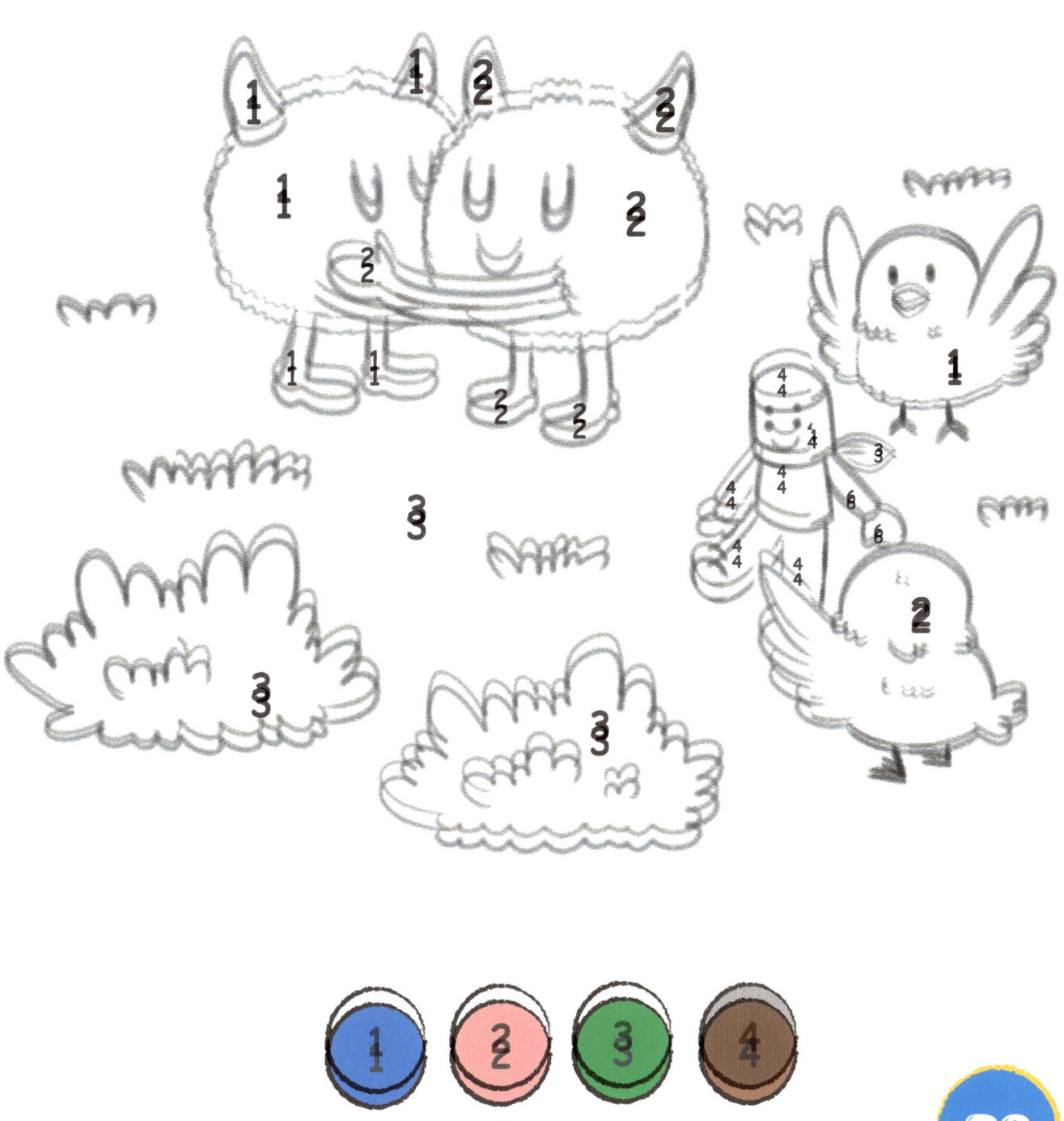

# Quincy's Determined Drive

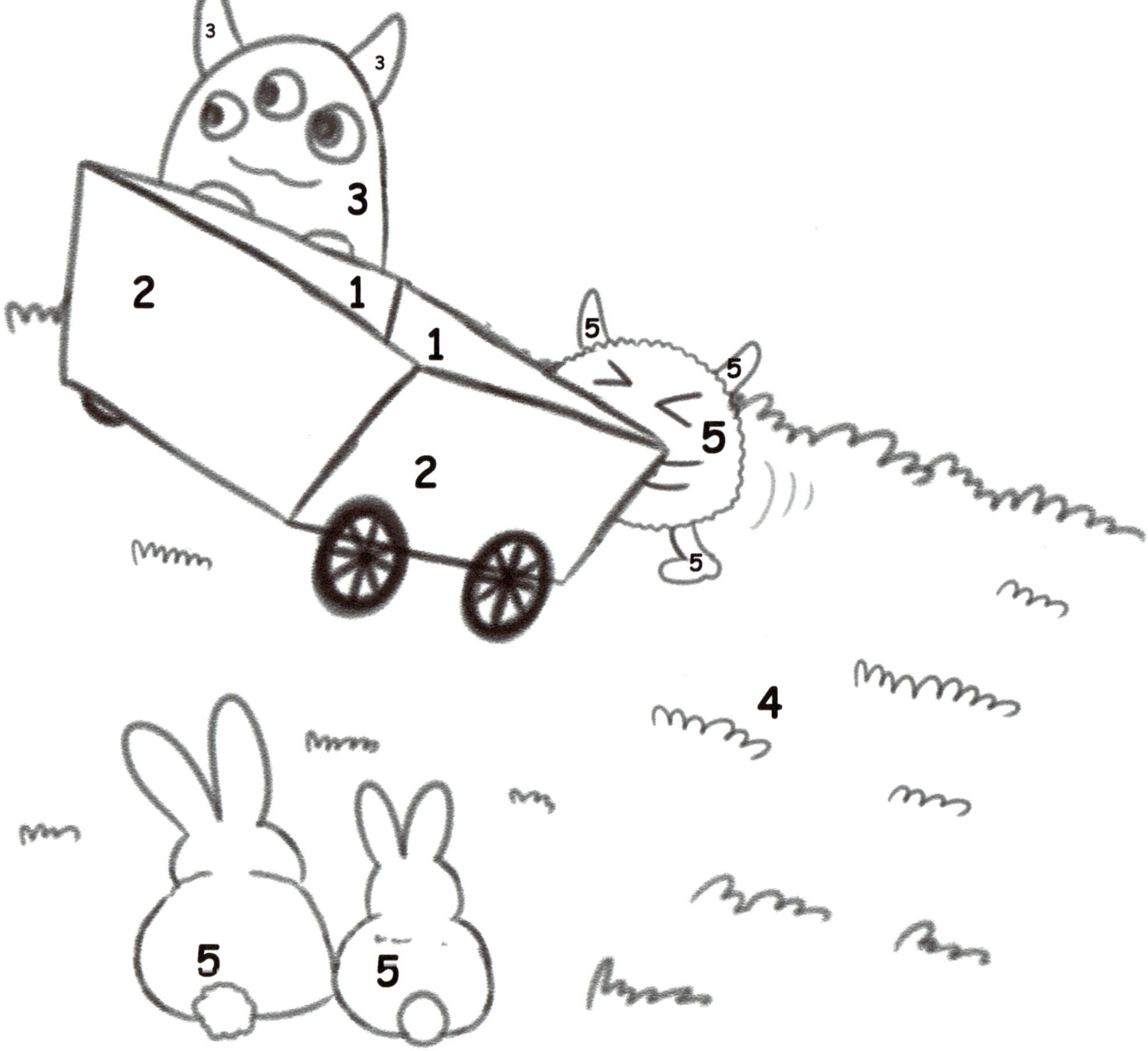

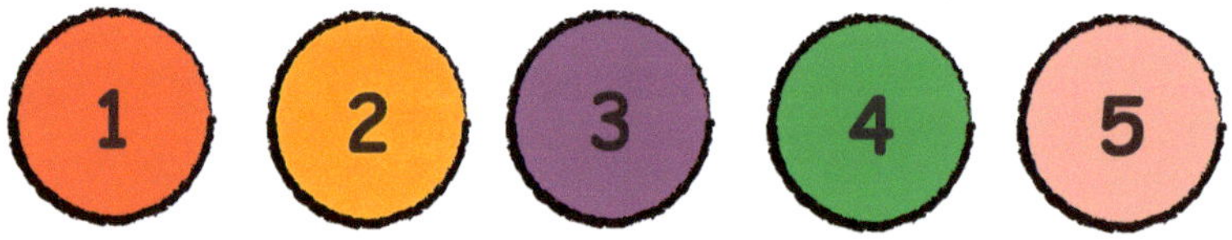

# Grandpa's Kindness Kite

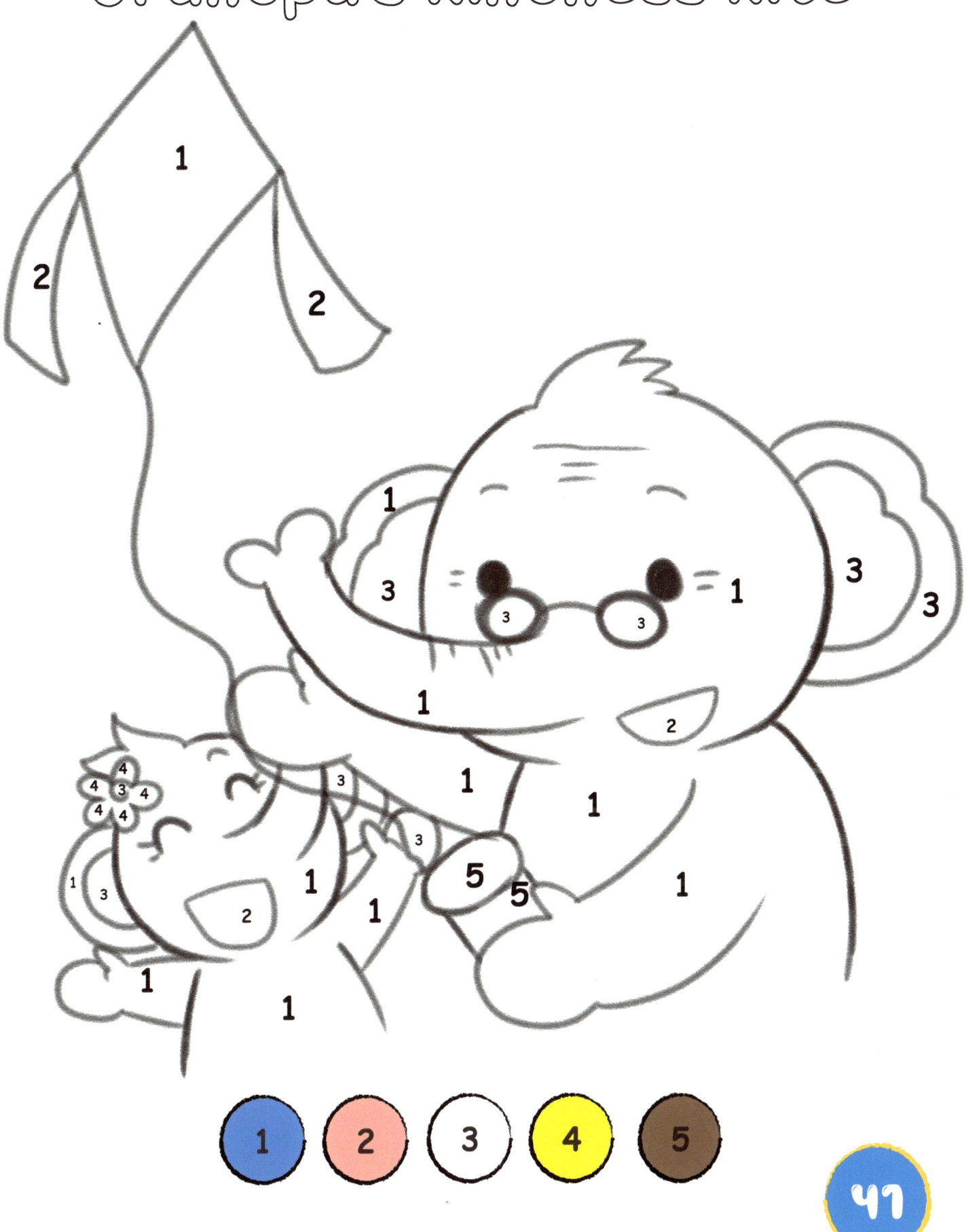

# Leigh's Encouraging Ensemble

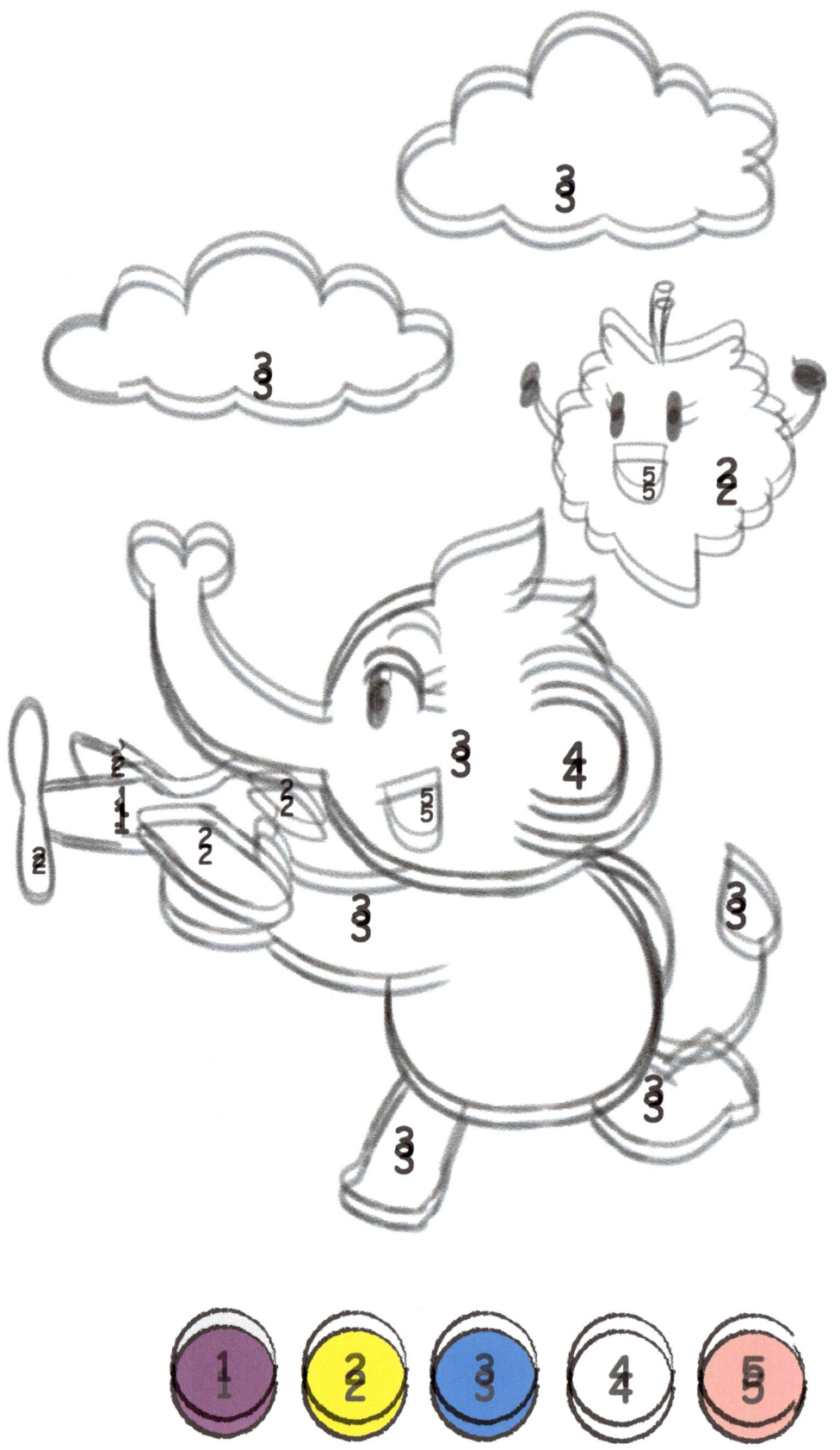

# Discover Emotional Intelligence Essentials

Equip children with the tools for emotional growth. Delve into our tailored resources that blend expertise with care, covering every facet of Social-Emotional Learning.

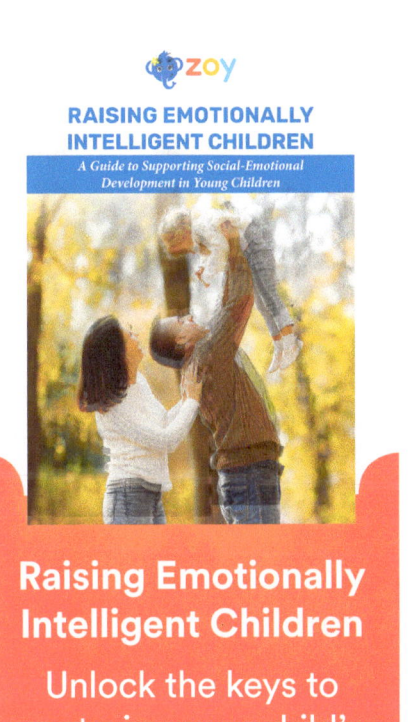

**Raising Emotionally Intelligent Children**

Unlock the keys to nurturing your child's emotional wellbeing and intelligence.

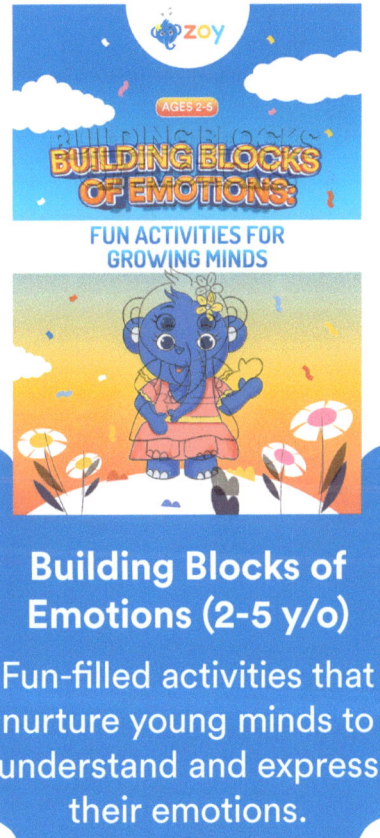

**Building Blocks of Emotions (2-5 y/o)**

Fun-filled activities that nurture young minds to understand and express their emotions.

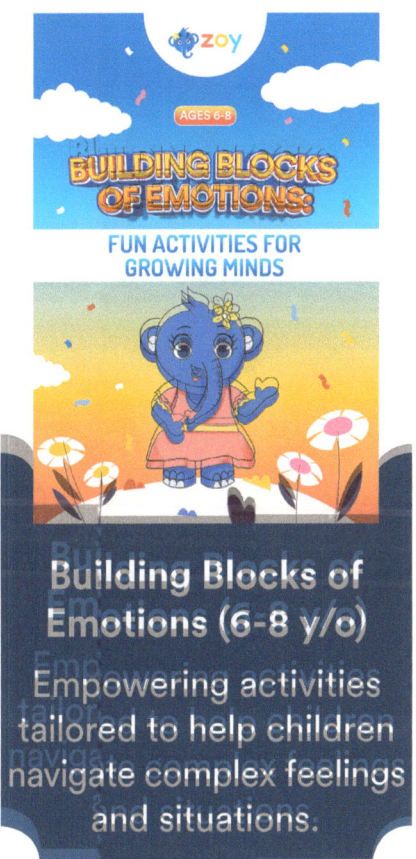

**Building Blocks of Emotions (6-8 y/o)**

Empowering activities tailored to help children navigate complex feelings and situations.

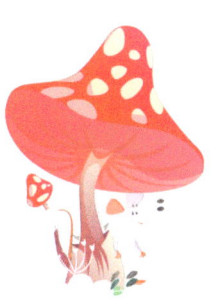

# A Treasury of Heartwarming Stories

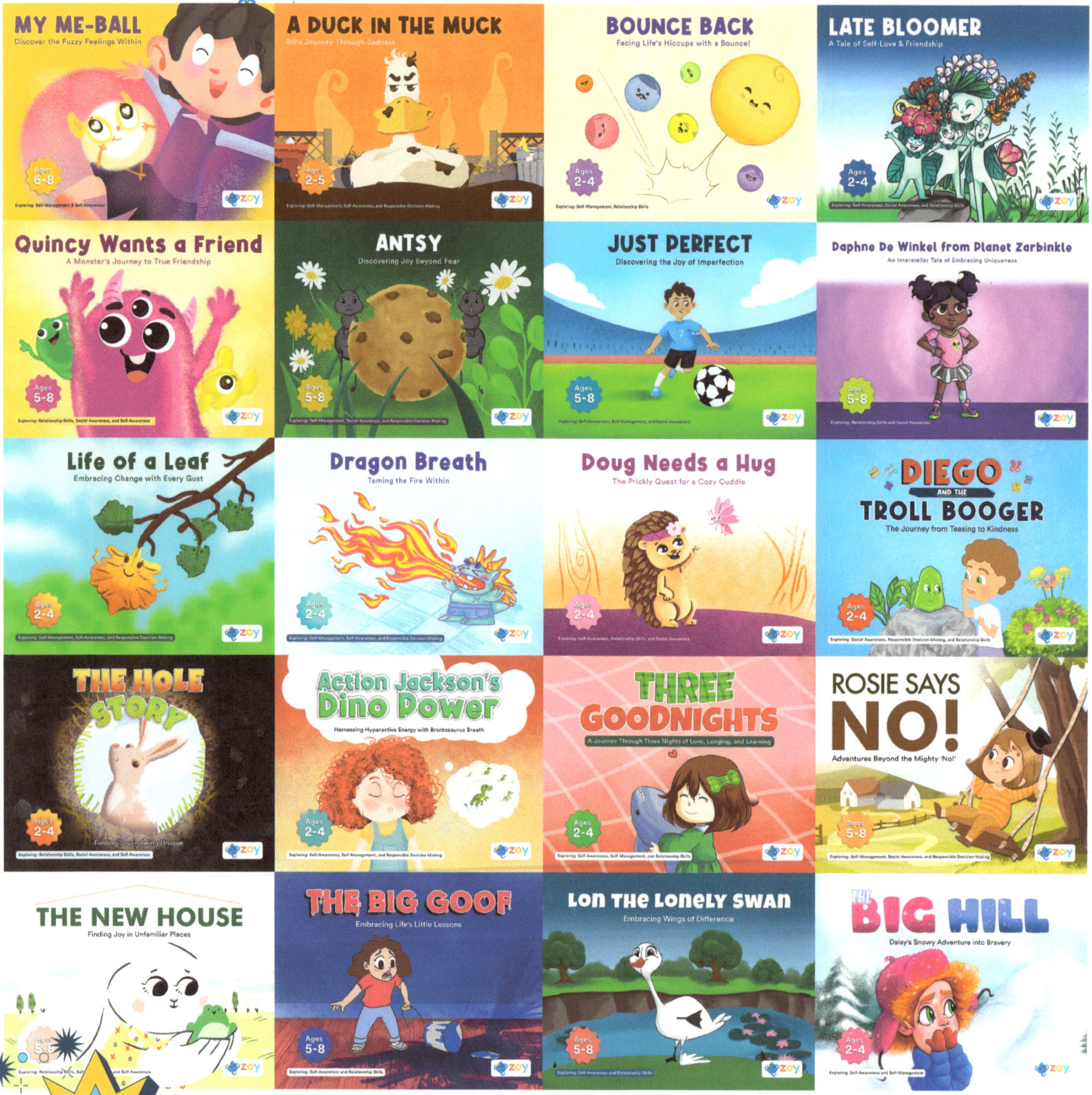

- **My Me-Ball** — Discover the Fuzzy Feelings Within (Ages 6-8)
- **A Duck in the Muck** — Bill's Journey Through Sadness (Ages 2-5)
- **Bounce Back** — Facing Life's Hiccups with a Bounce! (Ages 2-4)
- **Late Bloomer** — A Tale of Self-Love & Friendship (Ages 2-4)
- **Quincy Wants a Friend** — A Monster's Journey to True Friendship (Ages 5-8)
- **Antsy** — Discovering Joy Beyond Fear (Ages 5-8)
- **Just Perfect** — Discovering the Joy of Imperfection (Ages 5-8)
- **Daphne De Winkel from Planet Zarbinkle** — An Interstellar Tale of Embracing Uniqueness (Ages 5-8)
- **Life of a Leaf** — Embracing Change with Every Gust (Ages 2-4)
- **Dragon Breath** — Taming the Fire Within (Ages 2-4)
- **Doug Needs a Hug** — The Prickly Quest for a Cozy Cuddle (Ages 2-4)
- **Diego and the Troll Booger** — The Journey from Teasing to Kindness (Ages 2-4)
- **The Hole Story** — Finding Joy in Being Unique
- **Action Jackson's Dino Power** — Harnessing Hyperactive Energy with Brontosaurus Breath (Ages 2-4)
- **Three Goodnights** — A Journey Through Three Nights of Love, Longing, and Learning (Ages 2-4)
- **Rosie Says No!** — Adventures Beyond the Mighty 'No!' (Ages 5-8)
- **The New House** — Finding Joy in Unfamiliar Places
- **The Big Goof** — Embracing Life's Little Lessons (Ages 5-8)
- **Lon the Lonely Swan** — Embracing Wings of Difference (Ages 5-8)
- **The Big Hill** — Daisy's Snowy Adventure into Bravery (Ages 2-4)

**Explore More Titles in our App**

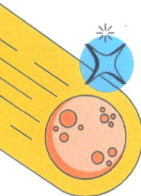

# A Treasury of Heartwarming Stories

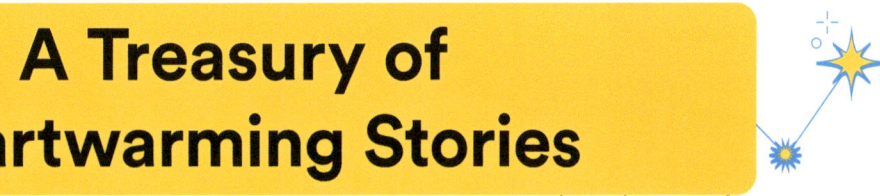

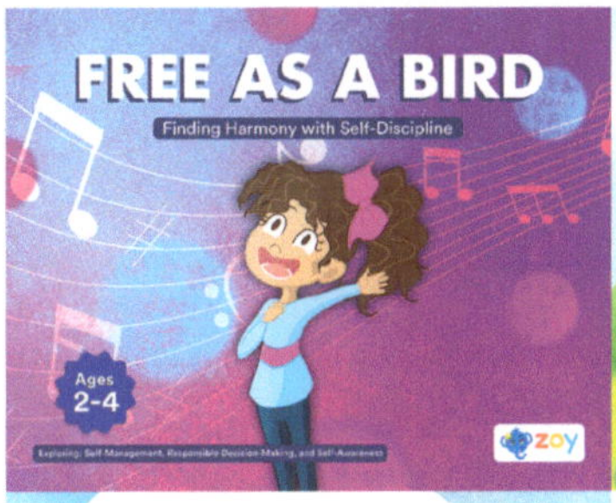

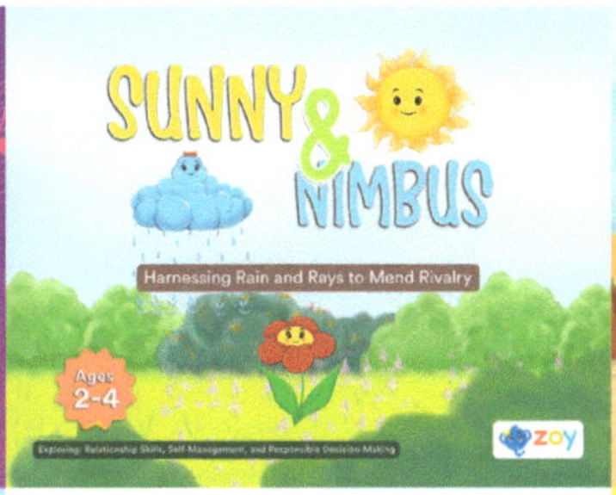

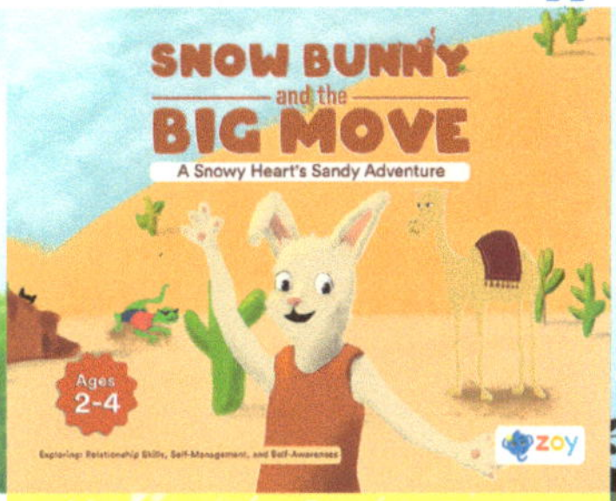

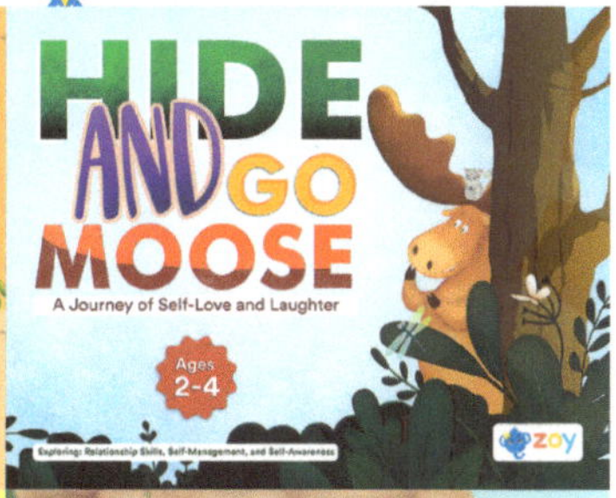

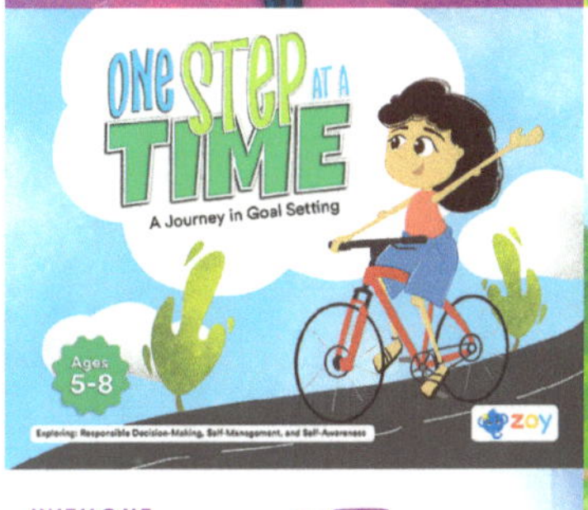

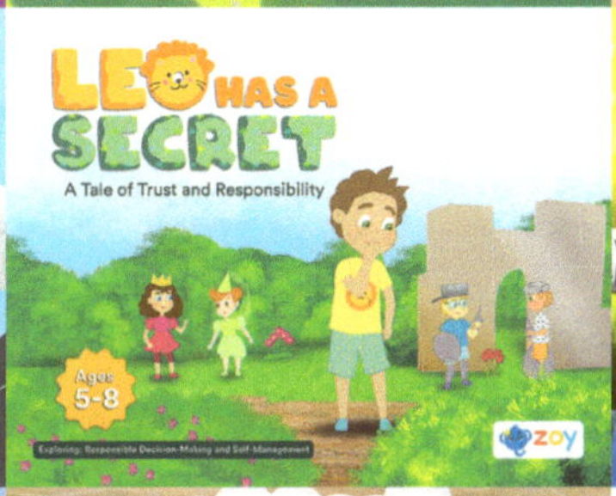

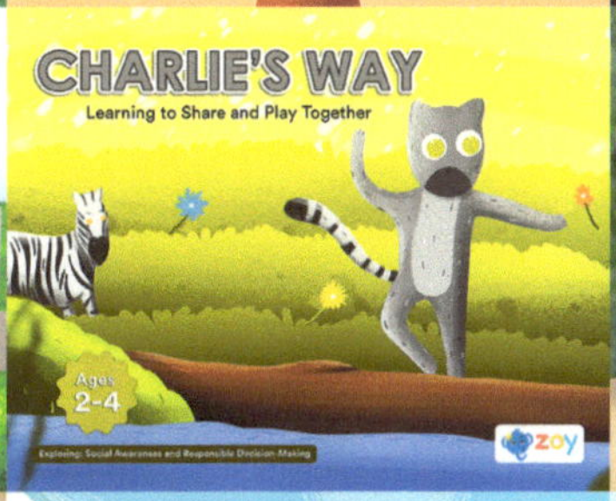

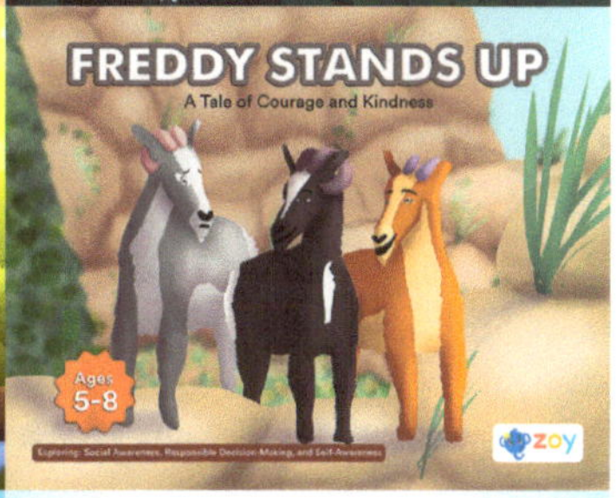

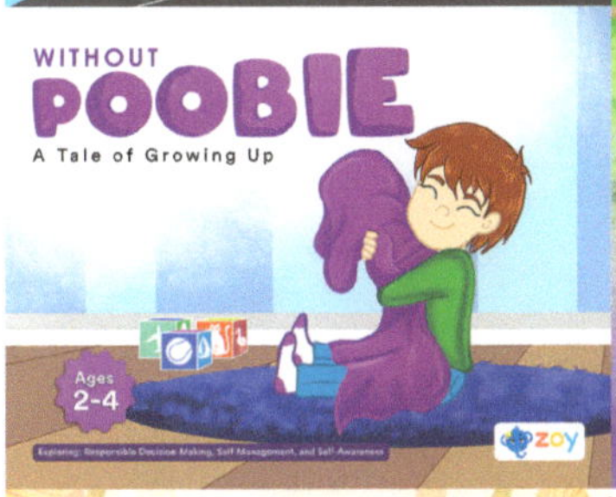

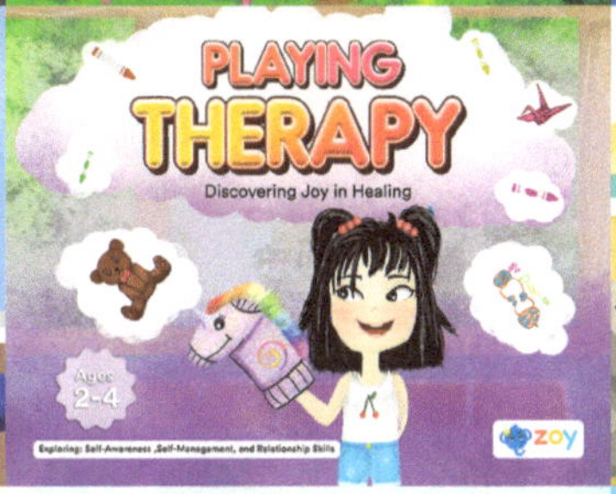

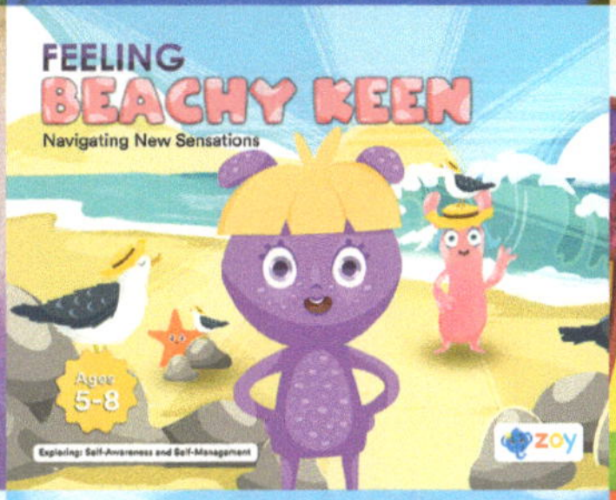

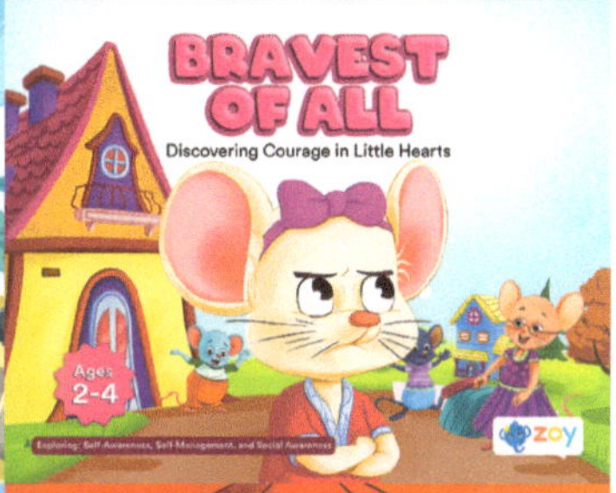

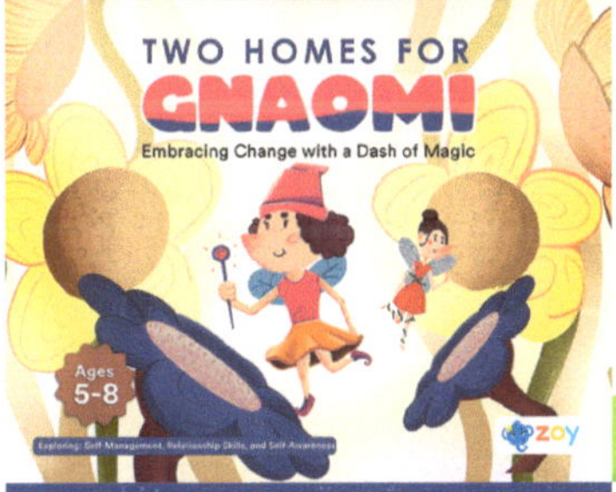

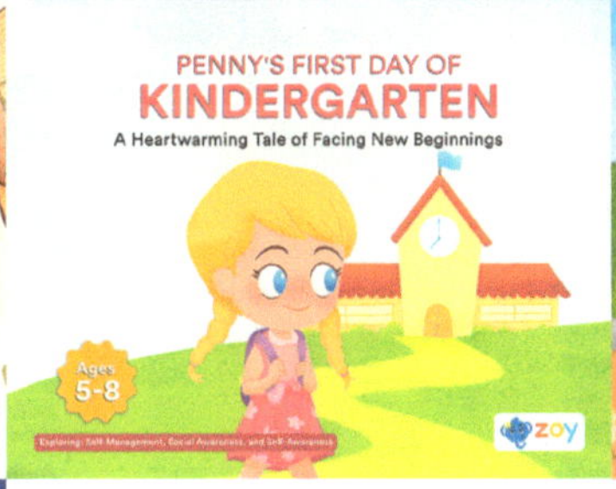

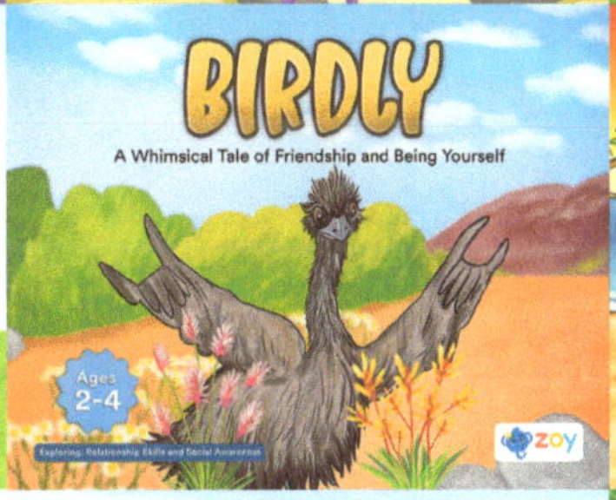

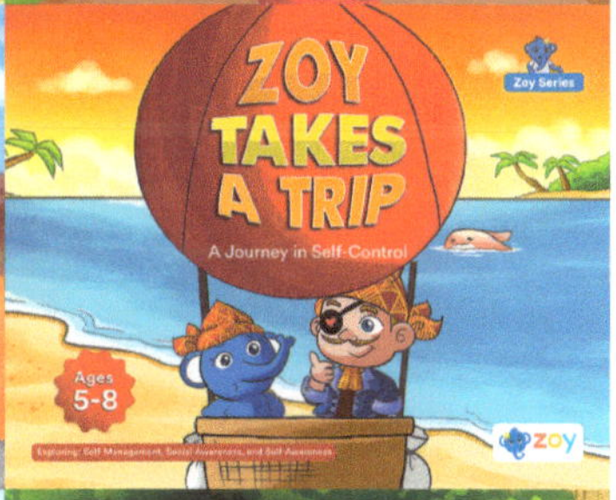

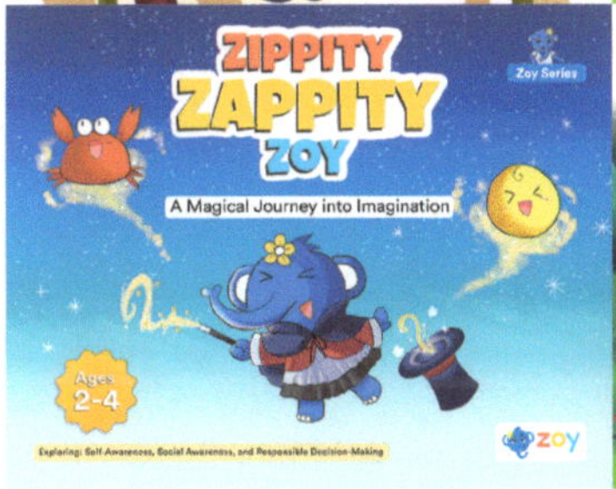

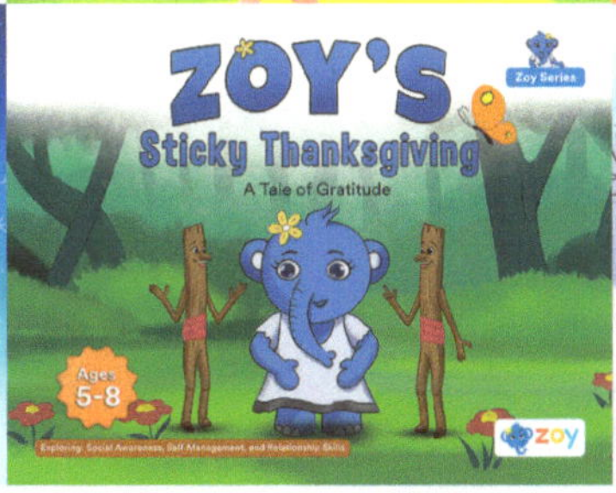

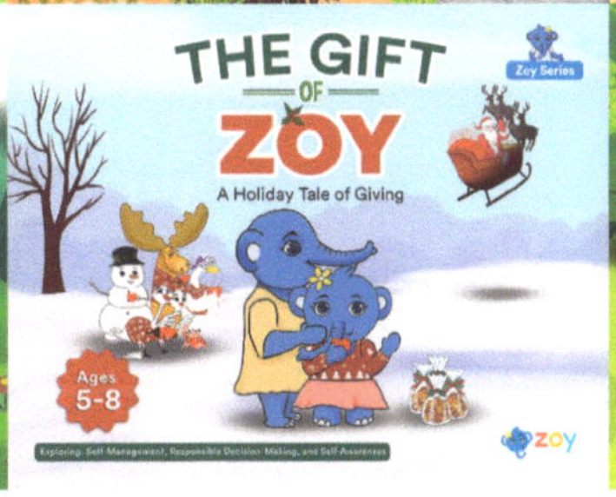

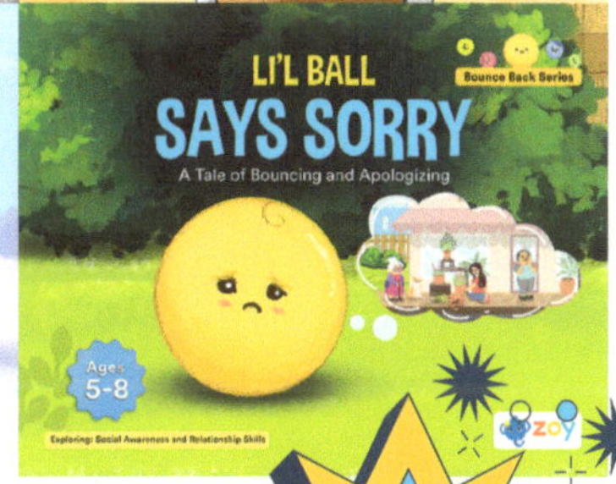

Explore More Titles in our App

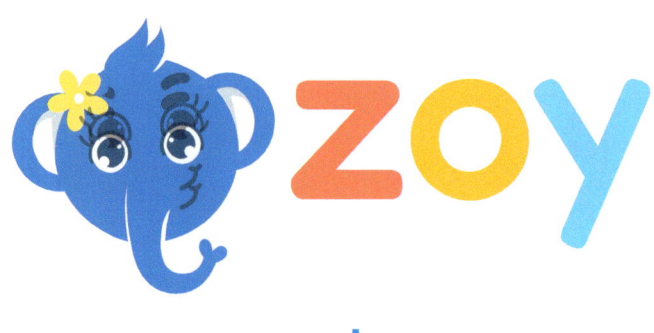

www.ingramcontent.com/pod-product-compliance
Lightning Source LLC
Chambersburg PA
CBHW051928210526
45473CB00006B/2174